Juice!

Juice!

Over 110 delicious recipes

Pippa Cuthbert &
Lindsay Cameron Wilson

Good Books®

Intercourse, PA 17534
800/762-7171
www.goodbks.com

Dedication – For the Jameses

First published in the United States by
Good Books
Intercourse, PA 17534
800/762 - 7171
www.goodbks.com

Text and photographs copyright © 2004 New Holland Publishers (UK) Ltd
Copyright © 2004 New Holland Publishers (UK) Ltd

JUICE!
Good Books, Intercourse, PA 17534
International Standard Book Number: 1-56148-425-3
(paperback edition)
International Standard Book Number: 1-56148-426-1
(comb-bound paperback edition)

Library of Congress Catalog Card Number: 2003025989

Library of Congress Cataloging-in-Publication Data

Cuthbert, Pippa.
    Juice! : over 100 delicious recipes / by Pippa Cuthbert and Lindsay
Cameron Wilson .
        p. cm.
Includes bibliographical references and index.
    ISBN 1-56148-425-3 (pbk.) -- ISBN 1-56148-426-1 (comb.-bound pbk.) 1.
Juicers. 2. Fruit juices. 3. Vegetable juices I. Wilson, Lindsay
Cameron. II. Title.
    TX840.J84C88 2004
    641.8'75--dc22
                            2003025989

Senior Editor: Clare Hubbard/Design: Paul Wright @ Cube/Photography: Ryno
Stylist: Justine Drake/Production: Hazel Kirkman/Editorial Direction: Rosemary Wilkinson

Reproduction by Pica Digital Pte Ltd, Singapore
Printed and bound in Malaysia by Tien Wah Press

Publisher's note
The information given in this book is not intended as a substitute for professional medical care. The publisher and authors do not represent or warrant that the use of recipes or other information contained in this book will necessarily aid in the prevention or treatment of any disease, and specifically disclaim any liability, loss or risk, personal or otherwise, incurred as a consequence, directly or indirectly, of the use and application of any of the contents of this book. Readers must assume sole responsibility for any diet, lifestyle and/or treatment program that they choose to follow. If you have questions regarding the impact of diet and health, you should speak to a healthcare professional.

The publishers have made every effort to ensure that the information contained in this book was correct at the time of going to press, but medical and nutritional knowledge are constantly evolving. The authors and publisher cannot be held liable or responsible for any form of misuse of any herb, herbal preparation or so-called herbal remedy. You should check with a qualified medical practitioner that the product is suitable for you.

Acknowledgments
Thanks to our friends at Books for Cooks for their support and inspiration.

The publishers and authors would like to thank New Classics for supplying the Waring juicers and blenders for photography (pages 11 and 12) and recipe testing.

Contents

Introduction

Juice! is the book for you if you lead, or want to lead, a healthy lifestyle. There are over 110 recipes for your juicing needs from morning until night. You will also find out things you never knew that you wanted to know about a whole host of fruits, vegetables and herbs. But, most of all, *Juice!* is about taste. Each recipe is a celebration of global flavors which, thanks to the abundance of wonderful ingredients now available, are accessible to us all.

We weren't always juice fanatics. Yes, there was a time when we innocently went about our lives thinking that a swig of juice from a carton was all the vitamin C we needed. We are, you see, food writers and stylists. We inhabit a world where aesthetics and the story behind food is paramount and health is a distant second. Even the cookbook shop where we met shares the same philosophy. The delicious, rich and succulent food books are displayed at the forefront, while books on healthy subject matters are tucked behind the front door. However, this was before we both bought juicers. Before we tasted sweet pomegranate juice. Before our cheeks glowed in the

dead of winter. Before we were addicted to the beauty of juice and its benefits.

Eating fruits and vegetables is a vital part of a healthy, balanced diet, with many health organizations and nutritionists recommending that you should eat at least five servings a day. Eating a banana in the morning is an easy task, but having another four servings is another thing altogether. Yet we discovered, as our love affair with juices developed, that our daily requirements were already being fulfilled, simply by

sipping on exquisite juice concoctions. Although the insatiable desire to explore uncharted flavor combinations was the initial driving force of our passion, the gifts that we received in the process became increasingly impossible to ignore. Soon we had thicker hair, glowing skin, cleansed bodies and boundless energy. Call us vain, but it was the "Wow, you look good" comments from those around us, that also kept the juices flowing.

Drinking fresh juices isn't a new idea. Doctors and naturopaths have been using fresh juices to treat patients since the nineteenth century. "Juicing for health" pioneers, who hailed from Germany and Switzerland in the late nineteenth and early twentieth centuries, devised the *Röhsaft Kur* (the fresh juice cure), which is still practiced today all over the world.

Then, many decades later in the late 1980s, the juicing craze hit California. Everyone was either setting up a juice bar or patronizing one. The success of juices in California is attributed to the abundance of local, fresh fruits, the "take-away" lifestyle and, most of all, the importance Californians place on health and their bodies. It wasn't long before this craze swept across the rest of the USA, through Canada, across Europe and down to Australia, New Zealand and South Africa. Today, juice bars – from über-trendy to naturally holistic – are everywhere. Juicing has become a way of life.

Taking a walk down the Edgware Road in London, home to countless Middle Eastern restaurants, makes you question the true origins of juicing. There, amidst the bubbling pipes, tabbouleh and lamb kofta on a skewer, are giant juicers filled with fruit. You wouldn't even think of sitting down to a plate of kibbee without a tall glass of cantaloupe juice at your side.

"Fruit and vegetable juices are an essential part of our drinking culture in the Middle East," says food writer

Anissa Helou. Juices are served from vendors along the streets, in cafés and in homes. When Helou was young, her mother would take her to the same café in Beirut every Saturday at noon, where she would perch on a stool and sip fresh carrot juice with her meal. "It wasn't a luxury item, it wasn't unusual, it was a healthy, refreshing part of daily life in a hot country."

Many of the juices in this book are inspired by the flavors of the Middle East and celebrate its juicing tradition. As Helou said, juicing is a familiar part of their daily life. Familiarity breeds habit, so why not place a juicer permanently on your kitchen counter so juicing can become a daily part of your life as well? Juicing at home gives you the freedom to experiment with a wide variety of fruits and vegetables, and to see, first hand, how they affect your body. As juicing becomes a regular part of your life, not only will your body become healthier, your senses will grow sharper. Every sip, depending on the fruit, the vegetable, the variety or the season, becomes an exciting taste sensation. Some flavors are explosive, others are mild. Some tingle, others glide. Textures can be frothy or so thin they dissipate across the tongue. These intriguing taste-tests, which we conducted, are the inspiration behind the descriptive word included with each recipe. Putting a single word to each flavor, however, wasn't always on the tip of the tongue. Flavors are often difficult to describe, says Mark Miller, an American food writer, restaurateur and chili pepper expert. He says, "Taste is an existential, sensual experience. We really don't understand it. Language is what we use for taste, and yet the body goes through this temporal process; there are highs and lows, intensities and durations. Taste is a very, very complex thing in the body." Using language to describe taste, Miller explains, is analytical, and not always about the experience itself. Our descriptive words are therefore mere guidelines – we will leave you to come up with your own once you've sampled your juices.

So, get started. Peel those bananas, chop the feijoas and deseed the melon, because juice has never tasted so good.

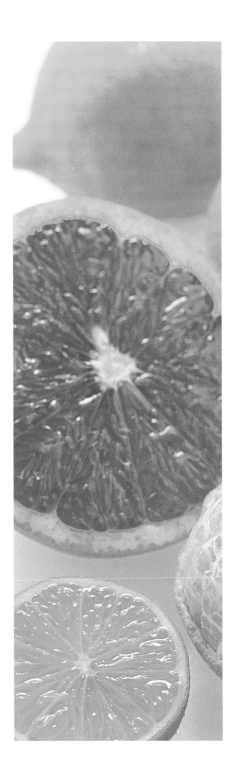

Juicers and blenders

Juicers aren't simply for health junkies or kitchen gadget lovers. Juicing is a quick and healthy habit that can be worked into your daily routine, regardless of how busy you are. The first thing you need to do is invest in the right equipment. Whether it's citrus fruits, carrots, wheatgrass or a blend of all three that you're after, there's a juicer or blender out there that's perfect for you. Note that for many of the recipes, you will need a juicer and a blender.

Quality costs

The higher the wattage of the juicer, the more efficient and expensive it will be. Wattage varies greatly from juicer to juicer. The first thing you need to do is decide what kind of juice you want. Do you want a pulpy, fast product or a crystal clear liquid? Do you want to juice dense, fibrous vegetables or soft, tender kiwis? The harder the grinding job, the more powerful and durable the juicer will need to be (think juicing a turnip versus a blackberry). Domestic juicers can have a wattage as low as 200, while industrial juicers can have well over 1000 watts. It is important to decide from the start how serious you are about juicing, keeping in mind that most of us don't need an industrial juicer strong enough to juice a small tree. Juicing is an investment in your health, which, of course, is priceless.

As well as considering how much you want to spend, there are a few other things to take into consideration:

• Always look out for a juicer with a stainless steel blade, not aluminium, which rusts more easily and can taint your food.

• Look for a feed tube that is at least large enough to fit a whole, large carrot. It's no fun chopping your fruits and vegetables into matchsticks in order to get them into the juicer.

• Look for a juicer with a cup large enough to accommodate at least 18fl oz (500ml) of juice.

• Make sure there is a sufficiently sized compartment in the juicer to collect pulp as you juice. Some juicers have an external container to collect pulp, which means you can juice longer without having to stop and de-clog.

Juicing methods

There are three basic types of juicer: centrifugal, masticating and press. Whatever type of juicer you have, always remember to clean it and your workspace thoroughly after use. A tidy kitchen results in a tidy mind – you will function more efficiently in your day and also inhibit the growth of any germs or bacteria.

Centrifugal juicers

Most, if not all, of the cheaper domestic juicers fall into this category. Centrifugal juicers work by

first grinding the fruit and vegetables, then spinning them at very high revolutions per minute (RPM), somewhat like a washing machine. The juice runs out and the pulp is ejected into a separate container.

Centrifugal juicers are not generally recommended if you want a high-quality juice on a daily basis. The end product is quite thick and cloudy, contains a lot of pulp, and enzymes can be destroyed in the juicing process. But, with the additional citrus and blender attachments often available with these juicers, they are an affordable way to start juicing.

Masticating juicers

These are the second most expensive type of juicer on the market. Masticating juicers operate at a slower speed than centrifugal juicers. They masticate by chewing up fruit and vegetable fibers and breaking down their cell structure. Masticating juicers perform better with fibrous fruit and vegetables than centrifugal juicers. The quality of the end product is high and more juice is removed from the pulp than from a centrifugal juicer. This produces a less cloudy juice, which is more nutritious as it retains more fiber, enzymes, vitamins and trace minerals in the finished product. More expensive masticating juicers often come with additional

homogenizing units that make baby foods, sauces and fruit sorbets.

Press juicers

Press juicers are the most efficient and, consequently, the most expensive juicers you can buy. Press juicers work by first crushing the fruit and vegetables and then pressing them, much like the press used to make extra virgin olive oil. They are typically the slowest of the juicers (turning at a slower RPM) which creates little friction; therefore no heat is applied to the fruit. Press juicers produce by far the best quality juice. The process gives you more fiber, enzymes, vitamins and trace minerals than any other method. The nutritional value of pressed juice is so high that it is often used as a medicinal

supplement for patients, especially those suffering from cancer. Some press juicers have the additional function of magnetic and bioceramic technology. This is beneficial as it slows down the oxidation process, meaning juices can be stored for longer (three days maximum).

Blenders

Blenders are generally cheaper than juicers. Hand blenders are also readily available on the market and require less cleaning. Blenders, as their name suggests, blend fruits and vegetables. They do not extract juice. If you prefer a thicker, pulpy, more textured fruit drink, then a blender is all you require. Yogurt,

milk and ice, along with other ingredients, can be added to blenders, and the end result is referred to as a smoothie, shake or ice crush. However, if pure juice is want you want, separated from pulp, a juicer is what you'll have to buy.

Additional juicing tools

In order to make your juicing experience as easy and as enjoyable as possible, we recommend investing in a few extra juicing tools.

Fine sieve or muslin – essential for straining unwanted pulp or ingredients.

Fine wire brush – for cleaning your juicer.

Glass jars with lids – these are great for storing and transporting juices. Don't forget to shake before drinking.

Lemon squeezer – essential for when a squeeze of lemon or dash of lime juice is required to stop oxidation and browning.

Measuring spoons and jugs.

Plastic milk/juice containers – recycle these for freezing "pure" juices, e.g. apple, pear, melon and tomato.

Scales – if you want to make juicing a science, then scales are essential. Don't forget you can and should be experimental while juicing – use

what is in season or what you have in your fridge. Make substitutions and adjust the recipes to suit your own taste buds – they are only a guide!

Scrubbing brush – make sure you remove all the dirt from your fruit and vegetables by washing or scrubbing.

Sharp knives – good, sharp knives are important in any kitchen and for any task. Make sure your knives are sharpened on a regular basis, preferably by the same person.

Small whisk – use to combine different juices.

Vacuum flask – this is the more expensive alternative to glass jars. Great for those Twelve pm: Hunger juices (see pages 38–61).

Vegetable peeler – use only when necessary. Most of the nutrients in fruits and vegetables are in the skin.

Standard weights

1 bunch ALFALFA SPROUTS	⅓oz/10g
1 APPLE cored and quartered	5oz/150g
1 APRICOT stoned	1⅔oz/50g
1 bunch ARUGULA	⅔oz/20g
1 AVOCADO peeled and stoned	4oz/125g
1 BANANA peeled	3½oz/100g
1 BEETROOT with leaves	3½oz/100g
1 handful BLACKBERRIES (fresh/frozen)	1⅔oz/50g
1 handful BLACKCURRANTS stalks removed (fresh/frozen)	1⅔oz/50g
1 handful BLUEBERRIES (fresh/frozen)	1⅔oz/50g
1 baby CABBAGE (red/white) outer leaves removed	14oz/400g
1 CARROT top and bottom removed	3½oz/100g
1 stalk CELERY trimmed, with leaves	1⅔oz/50g
1 CELERIAC peeled	10½oz/300g
1 handful CHERRIES stoned and stalks removed	1⅔oz/50g
1 head CHICORY	5½oz/160g
1 fresh CHILI	⅙oz/5g
1 bunch CORIANDER chopped	⅓oz/10g
1 handful CRANBERRIES (fresh/frozen)	1⅔oz/50g
1 CUCUMBER	1lb/500g
1 FEIJOA flesh scooped out	2½oz/75g
1 FENNEL bulb outer part removed	7¾oz/225g
1 FIG	1⅓oz/40g
1 clove GARLIC peeled	⅙oz/5g
½in (1cm) piece fresh GINGER peeled	⅙oz/5g
1 handful GOOSEBERRIES (fresh/frozen)	1⅔oz/50g
1 bunch GRAPES (red/white) stems removed	7oz/200g
1 GRAPEFRUIT (ruby red/white) peeled	7oz/200g
1 head ICEBERG LETTUCE outer leaves removed	1lb3¼oz/550g
1 KIWI FRUIT	2½oz/75g
1 LEEK trimmed	3½oz/100g
1 LEMON peeled	2½oz/75g
1 stalk LEMONGRASS trimmed and chopped	⅓oz/10g
1 LIME peeled	1⅔oz/50g
1 LYCHEE	⅓oz/10g
1 MANGE TOUT (snow peas)	1 tsp
1 MANGO peeled and stoned	7¾oz/225g
1 MELON (green/cantaloupe) peeled and deseeded	7oz/200g
1 NECTARINE stoned	2½oz/75g
1 ORANGE (blood orange) peeled	5oz/150g
1 PAPAYA peeled and deseeded	5oz/150g
1 bunch PARSLEY woody stalks removed	⅓oz/10g
1 PASSION FRUIT flesh scooped out	1oz/30g
1 PEACH stoned	5oz/150g
1 PEAR cored and quartered	5oz/150g
1 PEPPER (red/green) stalk removed, deseeded	4oz/125g
1 PERSIMMON peeled	2oz/60g
1 PINEAPPLE peeled	2lb/900g
1 PLUM (including greengage) stoned	1⅔oz/50g

1 POMEGRANATE

    seeds scooped out   3½oz/100g

1 QUINCE peeled and quartered 7oz/200g

1 head RADICCHIO

    outer leaves removed   2oz/60g

1 RADISH with leaves   ½oz/7.5g

1 handful RASPBERRIES

    (fresh/frozen)   1¾oz/50g

1 SAGE LEAF   1 tsp

1 bunch SPINACH

    tough stalks removed, chopped 1¾oz/50g

1 SPRING ONION trimmed   ⅓oz/10g

1 SQUASH

    peeled, deseeded   10½oz/300g

1 handful STRAWBERRIES

    hulled   3½oz/100g

1 SWEET POTATO peeled   7oz/200g

1 TAMARILLO flesh scooped out 1¾oz/50g

1 TOMATO stem removed   2½oz/75g

1 handful WATERCRESS   1¾oz/50g

1 WATERMELON

    flesh and seeds scooped out   4lb/2kg

1 handful WHEATGRASS

    rinsed and chopped   ⅓oz/10g

Reminders

• Each recipe makes 8fl oz (250ml) juice; this is one serving.

• Use organic produce whenever possible to avoid pesticide and herbicide residue. If you are not using organic ingredients, peel all fruits and vegetables first.

• Before juicing, wash all produce and remove any dirt, bruised or moldy bits, stalks, waxy, bitter peel, woody stems, stones, bitter greens and any other inedible elements before juicing. For detailed information on preparing fruits, vegetables and herbs, see pages 140–169.

• Fresh herbs should be used unless otherwise stated.

• Tbsp = tablespoon/tsp = teaspoon.

• See pages 170–172 for information on vitamins and minerals.

• Freshness is everything. Drink juices the day they are made as the nutritional value decreases the longer the juice is exposed to air. Keep stored in the fridge and drink within two to three days.

• Due to the slight risk of salmonella, juices containing raw eggs should not be served to children, the ill or elderly or to pregnant women.

• Children and pregnant or breast-feeding women should not take herbal remedies or supplements (see pages 164–169).

• If using herbal remedies or supplements always read the information supplied by the manufacturer to check that the product is suitable for you (see pages 164–169). If in doubt, consult a medical practitioner. Omitting the herbal supplements will not affect the deliciousness of the juice.

• If taking prescribed medication, consult your doctor before consuming large amounts of grapefruit juice.

• Those new to juice-drinking should start with no more than two servings a day. Gradually work your way up to a comfortable intake – a maximum of three to four servings a day. Vary your fruits and vegetables for maximum nutrient intake.

• Juices should always be diluted for children. Still mineral water is best, but you can use lemonade, sparkling water, soda or milk, where appropriate.

Seven am:

First thing in the morning is the best time to juice. That's when your body is an empty, willing vessel, ready and waiting to be filled with goodness. Hold off for now on the high octane java that will inevitably find its way inside later in the morning. You're a fresh, innocent flower, so shower yourself with goodness.

The following recipes make waking up a joy. Shuffle into the kitchen. Take out the juicer. Chop your fruits and vegetables to size. Toss them in. Don't forget to put the cup beneath the spout. This is where you might want to put on the earplugs – some juicers sound like a 747 about to take flight – and flick the switch.

Slowly pour the salubrious concoction into your mouth and feel it trickle down the esophagus. Allow a minute for the juice to take effect. Miraculously, your cheeks will begin to glow, a smile will appear and you will have a strange, insatiable desire to wash your juicer. Go with this. There's nothing worse than dried pulp at bedtime.

Wake-up call

Blueberry breakfast
orange | blueberry | yogurt | quinoa | olive oil | honey

Blueberry breakfast
Creamy

This breakfast drink is based on a cancer-fighting recipe developed by Dr Joanna Budwig, a six-time Nobel prize nominee. We swear by it.

---

1 **orange**
   peeled
2 handfuls **blueberries**
   (fresh or frozen)
4 Tbsp **live yogurt**
2 Tbsp **quinoa**
1 Tbsp **extra virgin olive oil**
1 Tbsp **runny honey**

Juice the orange and 1 handful of the blueberries together. Transfer to a blender. Add the remaining blueberries, yogurt, quinoa, oil and honey. Blend.

■ *Much of the fat in olive oil is in the form of monounsaturated fatty acids (MUFA), a type of fat, unlike saturated fat, that does not raise blood cholesterol levels.*

■ *The quality of proteins in quinoa is roughly equivalent to milk, because of its high concentration of amino acids.*

Apple spice
Spicy

For a winter warmer, heat this juice gently – the juniper berries will add color to your cheeks.

---

3 **apples**
   cored and quartered
Squeeze **lemon juice**
1 tsp **juniper berries**
   crushed

Juice the apples. Transfer to a blender and add the lemon juice and crushed juniper berries. Blend, then strain through a fine sieve or muslin. Serve cold or warm.

■ *Juniper berries help relieve indigestion, heartburn and bloating.*

■ *Apples are a delicious source of dietary fiber.*

Café cooler

Icy

If you are anything like us, coffee is essential in your morning routine. Try this instead – a healthy, balanced way to get your morning fix, plus other benefits as well.

1 **frozen banana**
   peeled and chopped
2 Tbsp **espresso**
1 Tbsp **maple syrup**
3½floz (100ml) **whole milk**

Blend all the ingredients thoroughly.

■ *Bananas are rich in fiber, potassium and vitamins C and B6.*

■ *Bananas take approximately 2 hours to freeze.*

■ *Espresso contains caffeine which is a diuretic and will help reduce water retention.*

Smooth ginger

Nectar

Banana and ginger are great friends and complement each other perfectly in this creamy, morning-munchie satisfier.

1 **banana**
   peeled
1 tsp **stem ginger syrup**
1 Tbsp **Manuka honey**
4 Tbsp **live yogurt**
3½floz (100ml) **whole milk**

Blend all the ingredients thoroughly.

■ *Yogurt is much more digestible than milk for those who suffer from lactose intolerance – the fermentation which produces yogurt converts most of the lactose in milk to lactic acid.*

■ *New Zealand's Manuka honey has strong antibacterial properties.*

Café cooler
banana | espresso | maple syrup | milk

Green ginger
melon | celery | ginger

Green ginger
Crisp

A crisp, refreshing palate cleanser with a warm ginger finish that will settle an upset stomach and soothe the digestive tract.

½ **green melon**
   peeled and deseeded
2 stalks **celery with leaves**
   trimmed
⅓in (1cm) **piece fresh ginger**
   peeled

Juice the melon. Juice the celery and ginger together. Combine.

■ *Celery juice, with its high concentration of sodium and potassium, is often recommended by naturopaths as an excellent natural remedy against arthritis and rheumatism.*

■ *Ginger is a well known anti-nausea remedy – an ideal treatment for morning sickness.*

Orange sunrise
Sweet

A spectacular blend of red, orange and yellow will add some sunshine to your day.

---

1 **orange**
   peeled
1 **lemon**
   peeled
3 **carrots**
   tops and bottoms removed
15 drops **echinacea extract**

Juice the orange and lemon together. Set aside. Juice the carrots. Pour the carrot juice and echinacea extract into the citrus juice mixture. Let the juices blend on their own.

■ *Carrots are one of the only vegetables that can be combined with fruit without causing flatulence.*

■ *Lemons have a gentle diuretic effect and help make this juice an effective cleanser.*

Barbie pink

Thick

This thick smoothie is shockingly reminiscent of Barbie's bubble-gum pink mini-van, but, something tells us Barbie didn't eat this well...

1 handful of **raspberries**
1 handful of **muesli**
3½fl oz (100ml) **live yogurt**
Squirt of **honey** to taste

Blend ingredients together.

■ *Instead of muesli, you can use any combination of the following: rolled oats, dried fruits, flax seeds, coconut, wheat bran and oat bran. Store in an air-tight container in the refrigerator.*

■ *Yogurt is made by adding fermenting agents* (lactobacillus bulgaricus *and* streptococcus thermophilus) *to milk that transform part of the lactose into lactic acid. When equal parts of the two bacteria are used, the environment is more active or "live." The more active the yogurt is, the healthier it is for the digestive system.*

Barbie pink
raspberry | muesli
yogurt | honey

Asian shot
Fresh

Our love of Asia and Asian ingredients inspired this juice. It is sweet and sour all in one.

3 **Comice pears**
   cored and quartered
1 handful **coriander**
   chopped
1 **lime**
   peeled

Juice the pears, coriander and lime together. Pour into a glass and add a sprig of fresh coriander.

■ *Coriander, also known as cilantro, is believed to help remove heavy metal toxins from the body – particularly mercury from dental fillings.*

■ *Pure lime juice has powerful antibacterial properties and may be applied directly to cold sores or spots.*

Grapefruit glory
Tart

A cool start to your day. Drink this half an hour before breakfast for your daily cleanse.

3 **grapefruit (see note, page 15)**
   peeled
8 **mint leaves**
6 **ice cubes**

Juice the grapefruit. Transfer to a blender and blend with the mint and ice.

■ *Mint owes its distinctive flavor and therapeutic properties to menthol, which leaves a fresh taste in the mouth and aids digestion.*

■ *Fruit juices, particularly the juices from citrus fruits, are stronger cleansers than vegetable juices and will speed the cleansing process.*

Wheatgrass wonder glass

Crisp

This truly is a wonder juice – wheatgrass has superpowers that perfectly complement the cleansing properties of celery and apple.

3 **apples**
   cored and quartered
1 stalk **celery with leaves**
   trimmed
1 handful **wheatgrass**
   rinsed and chopped

Juice the apples. Juice the celery and wheatgrass together. Combine.

■ *Wheatgrass is rich in chlorophyll, which purifies and enriches the blood.*

■ *Celery juice can help alleviate headache pain.*

Brainiac

Redolent

Kick-start your mind with this trio of flavors, filled with antioxidants that help combat cancer and heart disease.

2 **apples**
   cored and quartered
1 handful **wild blueberries**
1 handful **blackcurrants**

Juice the apples. Blend blueberries and blackcurrants with apple juice.

■ *3½oz (100g) of blueberries is packed with more antioxidant power than five servings of other fruits and vegetables.*

■ *Wild blueberries grow throughout eastern Canada and the northeastern United States. They are smaller, richer in flavor and have more health benefits than their cultivated cousins.*

Pear shape

Ethereal

This is a fiber-rich drink with the sweet aroma and taste of pear dominating your taste buds.

2 **pears**
   cored and quartered
1 **banana**
   peeled
Squeeze of **lemon juice**
15 drops **ginkgo biloba
   extract**

Juice the pears. Transfer to a blender with the banana and a squeeze of lemon juice. Add the ginkgo biloba.

■ *Ginkgo biloba is a favorite juice maximizer at Fresh, one of the oldest juice bars in Toronto. They promise it will increase dopamine, which aids in memory retention and mental alertness.*

■ *Ginkgo biloba has also been used in traditional medicine to treat circulatory disorders by dilating blood vessels and reducing the stickiness of blood platelets.*

Tropicana

Velvety

A thick, lush, tropical fruit salad in a glass. Have this for dessert if you prefer – even with a little frozen yogurt blended in, too.

1 **mango**
   peeled and stoned
1 **orange**
   peeled
1 **banana**
   peeled
6 **ice cubes**
1 **passion fruit**
   flesh scooped out

Juice the mango and orange together. Transfer to a blender and blend thoroughly with the banana and ice. Stir in the passion fruit flesh.

■ *Bananas are full of fiber and are a filling breakfast food all on their own.*

■ *Mangoes have more carotenoids than most fruits – and that helps to ward off colds and reduces the risk of cancer and heart disease.*

Flightless fuzzy

Tangy

Pippa, a New Zealander through and through, loves her kiwi fruit. This one's for her.

---

2 **kiwi fruit**
  peeled and halved
1 **orange**
  peeled and halved
1 **banana**
  peeled

Juice the kiwi fruit, then the orange. Combine the juices, then blend with the banana.

■ *Kiwi fruit are packed with vitamin C and aid in digestion.*

■ *The kiwi fruit, native to China, used to be called the "Chinese gooseberry" until production exploded in New Zealand. In 1953 it was renamed "kiwi" after a flightless, brown, fuzzy bird native to New Zealand.*

Pink lady

Zingy

Ruby red grapefruit give this drink its brilliant pink color and a sharp edge that will wake up any sleepy head.

---

1 **ruby red grapefruit (see note, page 15)**
  peeled
1 **white grapefruit (see note, page 15)**
  peeled
1 handful **cranberries**

Juice the grapefruit and cranberries together.

■ *The white pith of grapefruit contains pectin and bioflavonoids which make them an excellent antioxidant food.*

■ *Cranberries aid in the prevention and treatment of urinary tract infections.*

Pink lady
grapefruit | cranberry

Sesame street

Nutty

Tahini is a ground sesame paste which adds a Middle Eastern twist to this vibrant morning drink.

---

4 **carrots**
   tops and bottoms removed
1 tsp **tahini**
Juice of ½ a **lemon**
1 tsp **honey**
Sprinkle of **sesame seeds**
   (optional)

Juice the carrots. Blend with the tahini, lemon juice and honey, adding more or less to taste. Serve with a sprinkling of sesame seeds, if desired.

■ *Sesame, cultivated in Mesopotamia more than 3,500 years ago, was the first plant to be used for its edible oil.*

■ *Sesame seeds contain more oil than half their full weight. They aid in digestion, activate blood circulation and have laxative properties.*

Evergreen

Floral

Rosemary adds a delicious, slightly sophisticated dimension to sweet pear and apple juice.

---

1 **pear**
   cored and quartered
1 **apple**
   cored and quartered
1 sprig **fresh rosemary**
   needles removed

Juice the pear, then the apple. Blend with rosemary needles until finely chopped.

■ *Rosemary is one of those perfect herbs that is exquisitely aromatic, flavorful, acts as a herbal cure-all, makes delicious honey and, as we've discovered when used sparingly, tastes fabulous in juice.*

■ *Pears are best juiced when slightly underripe. If they're too firm, leave to ripen at room temperature away from other fruits – they produce lots of ethylene gas and will ripen the other fruits in the bowl as well.*

Sharon's drink

Mellow

Persimmons, also known as "sharon" in Israel or "kaki" in Japan, produce a deliciously creamy, mellow, sweet juice that pairs perfectly with wintery spices.

1 **persimmon**
  peeled, halved and deseeded
3 Tbsp **live yogurt**
1 pinch of **cinnamon**
1 pinch of **nutmeg**

Juice the persimmon and blend with the live yogurt. Add cinnamon and nutmeg to taste.

■ *Persimmons are a winter fruit. Their shiny, bright orange skin resembles tomatoes, but inside their flesh is sweet and firm; their seeds are inedible.*

■ *Persimmons are a good source of vitamins A and C and contain potassium and copper. They also have a mild laxative effect on the body.*

Sharon's drink
persimmon I yogurt
cinnamon I nutmeg

Morning loosener
pear | apple | prune

Morning loosener
Sweet

Ignore the negative stigma associated with prunes – this drink is nutritious, delicious and we love it.

---

2 **pears**
   cored and quartered
1 **apple**
   cored and quartered
8 **prunes**

Juice the pears and apple together. Transfer to a blender and add the prunes. Blend thoroughly.

■ *Prunes will have a laxative effect on your digestive system if you consume too many. Restrict this drink to one serving a day.*

■ *Pears and apples both contain large amounts of the soluble fiber pectin, which aids digestion and will provide you with instant energy.*

Sunshine
Tart

The addition of blended banana to any drink creates the illusion of a dairy product. This creamy but cream-less texture, combined with tart raspberries, orange and crisp mint makes for a smooth, rich, colorful start to your day.

---

2 **oranges**
   peeled and halved
1 handful **raspberries**
1 **banana**
   peeled
3 **mint leaves**

Juice the oranges. Blend with remaining ingredients and add a few ice cubes if desired.

■ *Fresh mint grows profusely in the garden, so much so it's best planted in a pot before being placed in the ground. Once clipped, it stays fresh in the refrigerator for several days.*

■ *Juicing oranges with the pith adds more antioxidants to the mix. It also creates a frothier, slightly tart juice.*

Suspended passion
orange | banana | passion fruit

Suspended passion

Fragrant

Passion fruit seeds, with their all-consuming floral aroma, gently float through this light and foamy juice.

2 **oranges**
  peeled and halved
1 **banana**
  peeled
1 **passion fruit**
  pulp scooped out

Juice the oranges. Blend with the banana and stir in the passion fruit pulp.

■ *Passion fruit is ripe when its skin becomes wrinkly like a raisin. When ripe, cut open and scoop out the sweet seeds. The seeds can be blended, but this breaks them up and leaves little black bits on the bottom of your glass.*

■ *Passion fruit is a good source of beta-carotene, calcium and is very cleansing to the digestive tract.*

Creamy nutmeg

Warming

We often add a raw, organic egg (see note, page 15) to this morning booster for extra fortification, but not everyone is keen on downing a raw egg. It's entirely up to you.

2 **bananas**
  peeled
4fl oz (125ml) **whole milk**
⅛ tsp **nutmeg**
  freshly grated

Blend bananas with milk and nutmeg.

■ *Nutmeg lends a warm flavor on its own, as well as being a wonderful flavor enhancer. Keep whole nutmeg in storage and grate as you need it – powdered nutmeg is a mere shadow of its former self.*

■ *Eggs are among the most nutritious foods on earth.*

Vampire juice

Vibrant

The color of this juice wavers on the edge of creepiness, but the flavor – with a shot of vinegar for zing and green algae for stamina – is amazing.

2 beetroot with leaves
2 stalks of celery
  trimmed
1 apple
  cored and quartered
½ tsp vinegar
Shot of green algae

Juice the beetroot, celery and apple separately. Blend with remaining ingredients.

■ Green algae – a fresh water seaweed – wards off cancer by arming the body with defensive natural killer cells that act on cancer cells as soon as they develop.

■ Vinegar can be made using a wide range of raw materials. We recommend using cider vinegar in this recipe.

Vanilla filler

Creamy

Choose free-range eggs whenever possible. Their yolks are sunflower yellow and enhance the appearance of this drink ten-fold.

1 banana
  peeled
1 vanilla pod
  seeds scooped out
1 tsp wheatgerm
1 egg (see note, page 15)
6 Tbsp live yogurt

Blend all the ingredients thoroughly.

■ A healthy vanilla pod will remain potent for as long as four years.

■ Wheatgerm is an extract of wheat and is often used as a dietary supplement because it's high in vitamin B.

Vanilla filler
banana | vanilla | wheatgerm | egg | yogurt

Twelve pm:

Lunchtime is when our stomachs grumble while our watches tick. We have the ever-present quandary of what interesting, nutritious food we can have. Then reality sets in and we march into a convenience store and help ourselves to a sandwich.

Nothing will change the need for fast nourishment, but there is something that can augment it – juice. Blitz your juice in the morning, pour it into a travel cup or flask and put it in the fridge once you get to work. When hunger strikes, give it a good shake, send the luscious pulp flying and wash away your sandwich blues.

Some of the recipes in this chapter are filling enough all by themselves. Others are designed to complement your meal. There are thick cleansing juices, sweet, antioxidant-rich fortifiers and gentle yet savory, cooling concoctions. Herbal remedies are scattered throughout the recipes. These can be added or left out at your discretion. It all depends on your early morning efforts, your taste and your appetite.

Hunger

Avocado ice
iceberg lettuce | lime | cucumber | avocado | wasabi

Avocado ice
Creamy

A liquid, Japanese-inspired guacamole on ice – nutritiously delicious and refreshing. We love it.

¼ **head iceberg lettuce**
   outer leaves removed
1 **lime**
   peeled
¼ **cucumber**
½ **avocado**
   peeled and stoned
1 tsp **wasabi (optional)**
3 **ice cubes**

Juice the lettuce, lime and cucumber. Transfer to a blender and blend with the avocado and wasabi. Serve over ice.

■ *Avocados are the most energy dense and nutrient-rich fruit per calorie.*

■ *Wasabi, which is also called Japanese horseradish, is available in speciality stores and Asian markets in both paste and powder form. It has a hot, fiery, pungent flavor. Take care.*

Beetroot zinger
Earthy

Beetroot and ginger are a delicious combination – earthy and zingy all in one.

---

2 **beetroot with leaves**
⅕in (0.5cm) piece **fresh ginger**
   peeled
2 **carrots**
   tops and bottoms removed
1 **orange**
   peeled

Juice all the ingredients and combine.

■ *The pigments in beetroot are much more stable than most red plant colors and are sometimes extracted and used as edible food coloring. Be careful not to stain your clothing.*

■ *Don't panic if your urine turns pink after consuming a lot of beetroot. It's harmless and it will soon return to normal when your intake falls.*

Grasshopper

Aniseed

Grasshopper green and super clean – you will feel extra healthy and more alert for the afternoon's activities.

1 **fennel bulb**
   outer part removed
2 stalks **celery with leaves**
   trimmed
1 **apple**
   cored and quartered
1 handful **wheatgrass**
   rinsed and chopped

Juice the fennel and celery together. Juice the apple with the wheatgrass. Combine.

■ *Did you know that you can buy male and female fennel bulbs? Look out for the less curvaceous male bulb for a sweeter and more tender product.*

■ *Wheatgrass is the blade that grows from spelt wheat, an ancient grain traditionally cultivated in Germany and Switzerland.*

Rejuvenator

Peppery

The Rejuvenator helps maintain oral hygiene and protects your gums from disease – all that, plus a peppery finish.

6 **radishes** with leaves
1 **lemon**
   peeled
3 **carrots**
   tops and bottoms removed

Juice all the ingredients together. Stir.

■ *The bitter flavor of radishes stimulates saliva flow – crucial in maintaining healthy gums.*

■ *The antibacterial properties of lemon help protect the mouth area and gums from cold sores and ulcers.*

Rejuvenator
radish | lemon | carrot

Hot recharge
yellow pepper | red pepper | chili | spinach

Hot recharge

Fiery

If you need a recharge, then look no further than this juice. If you can't handle the heat, dilute with a little splash of still mineral water.

---

1 **yellow pepper**
   stalk removed, deseeded
1 **red pepper**
   stalk removed, deseeded
1 **red chili**
   seeds and membrane
   removed
1 **bunch spinach**
   tough stalks removed,
   chopped

Juice the yellow pepper. Juice the red pepper and chili together. Finally, juice the spinach and add to the pepper juices. Stir before drinking.

■ *Yellow and red peppers are much sweeter than green peppers.*

■ *Chilies have a chemical effect on our bodies – they stimulate the appetite and cool the body.*

Sprout man

Peppery

Cress or any other peppery sprout can be used instead of alfalfa sprouts. You could even try arugula – it makes a delicious drink, too.

---

2 **apples**
   cored and quartered
2 stalks **celery with leaves**
   trimmed
1 handful **alfalfa sprouts**
Squeeze **lemon juice**

Juice the apples, celery and sprouts. Stir in the lemon juice.

■ *Alfalfa sprouts are one of the most complete and nutrient rich of all foods.*

■ *Apples are rich in quercetin, a natural antihistamine that is thought to reduce the risk of asthma attacks.*

Hot beets
beetroot | celery | garlic | carrot

Hot beets

Hot

Drink this juice after, not before, your lunch. Garlic can be a conversation killer, but it does have properties to help soothe the stomach when suffering from indigestion.

2 **beetroot** with leaves
1 stalk **celery with leaves**
   trimmed
2 **cloves garlic**
   peeled
2 **carrots**
   tops and bottoms removed

Juice all the ingredients. Combine.

■ *Garlic acts as a natural antibiotic and helps prevent colds and flu.*

■ *Be sure to include the green leafy tops of the beetroot if available. They are especially nutritious and contain calcium, beta-carotene and iron.*

Fennel fetish

Peppery

If you're not a huge fennel fan you may want to up the apple and reduce the fennel. It's up to you.

1 **fennel bulb**
   outer part removed
2 handfuls **watercress**
20 **mange-tout**
   chopped
1 **apple**
   cored and quartered

Juice all the ingredients together. Stir to combine.

■ *Fennel stimulates the liver and helps aid digestion.*

■ *Watercress has been continuously popular since ancient times. The Romans and Anglo-Saxons both ate watercress to avert baldness.*

Tamarillo tango

Tangy

The tamarillo is also known as the "tree tomato" and has a very unusual and distinctive flavor. This juice is based on an old tamarillo and orange sauce recipe. It works perfectly as a drink, too.

1 **orange**
  peeled
1 **tamarillo**
  flesh scooped out
6 Tbsp **live yogurt**
1 pinch **ground cinnamon**

Juice the orange. Transfer to a blender and blend with the tamarillo, yogurt and cinnamon. Shake well before drinking.

■ *Tamarillos are high in vitamin C and a good source of beta-carotene.*

■ *New Zealand is one of the largest producers of tamarillos in the world. Formerly known as "tree tomatoes," they were given a sexy new name in 1967 by New Zealand producers for export purposes.*

Maple butter

Sweet earthy

Butternut squash, a sweet, smooth winter squash, is delicious roasted with thyme and maple syrup. We imagined these flavors in a glass, *et voilà*, a divine drink was born.

10½oz (300g) **butternut squash**
  peeled and chopped
1 tsp **maple syrup**
1 Tbsp **fresh thyme leaves**
3½fl oz (100ml) **whole milk**

Juice the squash. Blend with remaining ingredients and drink immediately, while bits of thyme are suspended throughout.

■ *Maple syrup is made by reducing the sap of maple trees native to North America – mainly Quebec, Vermont, Maine, New York and Nova Scotia.*

■ *Butternut is a sweet, winter squash. It is much bigger than, but has a similar shape to, a pear. Its smooth skin is easy to peel, making it easier to juice.*

Maple butter

butternut squash | maple syrup | thyme | milk

Pis-en-lit

Bitter

Pis-en-lit, meaning "wet the bed" is what the French call dandelions – a comment on their diuretic effectiveness!

1 head **chicory**
2 **apples**
  cored and quartered
6 **dandelion leaves**
Squeeze **lemon juice**

Juice the first three ingredients together. Add the lemon juice.

■ *Dandelions act as a liver tonic by flushing out the system. This is ideal to consume after lunch as it also aids digestion. It is not a great idea to drink this juice before bed as the diuretic effect of the dandelion leaves doesn't take long to play its part.*

■ *Chicory is also known as endive, witloof and radicchio.*

Watermellow

Clean

Watermelon produces a delicate juice which we enhance at noon-time with a touch of mint and ginger.

1lb (500g) piece of **watermelon**
  peeled
Handful of **fresh mint**
1 tsp **stem** (or fresh) **ginger**
  chopped

Juice the watermelon, then blend with the remaining ingredients.

■ *Stem ginger is peeled ginger preserved in syrup. Once opened, store in the refrigerator.*

■ *In Juicing for Health Caroline Wheater explains that melon juice passes through the digestive system fastest, restricting the absorption of other juices. She suggests drinking watermelon juice alone for maximum health benefits. But for maximum taste, mix away.*

Watermellow
watermelon | mint | ginger

Terracotta

sweet potato | orange | banana

Terracotta
Creamy

This thick juice, although earthy in color, tricks the tongue with a mysterious strawberry-like flavor.

1 **sweet potato**
chopped
1 **orange**
peeled and halved
1 **banana**
peeled

Juice the sweet potato and orange. Blend with the banana.

■ *Sweet potatoes are often confused with yams. They are slightly sweeter and longer than yams and are happiest when their sweetness is encouraged: in pies, mashed and topped with brown sugar, caramelized in the oven or juiced with fruits.*

■ *Sweet potatoes are a great source of vitamins A, C, B6 and folic acid.*

Garden salad
Crisp

If you can get past the murky color of this juice you will realize just how good a garden salad in liquid form can taste.

2 stalks **celery with leaves**
trimmed
2 **tomatoes**
stalks removed
¼ **cucumber**
1 pinch **black pepper**

Juice the celery, tomatoes and cucumber. Stir in the pepper.

■ *Tomatoes are rich in lycopene, the antioxidant phytochemical which is important in helping to prevent heart disease and cancers.*

■ *Piperine, a component of black peppercorns and jalapeño peppers, is what gives them their fiery taste.*

Stigma
celeriac | celery | saffron

Stigma

Gentle

Juicing a brain-like bulb of celeriac produces an amazing amount of juice and adds a wonderful richness to celery. Saffron ties up the package with a sophisticated bow.

½ head **celeriac**
  scrubbed well and chopped
3 stalks **celery**
  trimmed
Pinch of **saffron**
  soaked in 1 tsp hot water

Juice the celeriac, then celery and blend together. Stir in saffron and its liquid.

■ *Never judge a root by its cover – celeriac may be ugly, but it is a flavorful source of potassium, vitamins C and B6, magnesium and iron. It cleanses the system and stimulates the appetite.*

■ *Saffron, the most ancient of spices, is the stigma of a crocus which is handpicked and dried; hence the high price. Saffron powder is also available, but it's never quite as nice.*

Zumo picante

Hot

Juicing tomatoes can be traumatizing. Unlike the rich-red store-bought stuff, a juiced tomato becomes a pale, murky pink color. But don't despair – the flavor is fresh and unquestionably superior, especially with a hit of onion and a dash of heat.

---

6 **tomatoes**
  stalks removed and quartered
2 **spring onions**
  chopped, white tips
  discarded
Dash of **Tabasco**
1 stalk **celery**
  trimmed

Juice the tomatoes. Blend with spring onions. Add a dash of Tabasco to taste and serve with a stalk of celery.

■ *Overripe tomatoes don't juice well and often have lost their flavor. Choose fragrant, firm tomatoes, ideally fresh from the vine.*

Electric raita

Softly sour

There are many flavor variations of raita, the traditional yogurt accompaniment to Indian dishes. Juiced cucumbers are pungent in flavor and electric in color, and when combined with lime and yogurt, the result of this combination is soft but sour. Of course we've thinned it a little to transport it from bowl to glass.

3½oz (100g) piece of **cucumber** chopped into chunks
3 **mint leaves**
Juice of ½ a **lime**
3½fl oz (100ml) **live yogurt**
Twist of **black pepper**

Juice the cucumber. Blend with remaining ingredients, adding pepper to taste.

■ *Cucumbers have a very high water content, which aids in the digestion of water-soluble vitamins.*

Jewels

Decadent

In the beauty bar at London's Harvey Nichols store, they wash hair with pomegranate juice; Nigella Lawson prefers them glistening over grilled eggplant. We like to drink them, strained, not shaken.

1 **pomegranate** halved and deseeded
1 **passion fruit** halved and pulp scooped out
3 Tbsp **live yogurt**

Carefully blend the pomegranate seeds, then strain through a fine mesh strainer. Stir in passion fruit pulp and yogurt.

■ *Pomegranate skins are extremely bitter, so never toss a whole pomegranate into a juicer. Instead, cut them in half, tap out the seeds, blend, then strain.*

Jewels
pomegranate | passion fruit | yogurt

Liquid thai
carrot | coriander | coconut milk

Liquid thai

Creamy

Unfortunately we can't serve this juice in true Thai style (plastic bags, roadside), but if you close your eyes and sip, you're practically there.

2 **carrots**
   tops and bottoms removed
1 handful of **coriander**
4fl oz (125ml) **coconut milk**

Juice the carrots. Blend with coriander and coconut milk.

■ Coconut milk is not the liquid floating around in the center of the nut, but a mix of grated, unsweetened coconut flesh heated with water or scalded milk, then strained. This can be made at home or bought canned.

Fruity guinness

Bitter sweet

Combining ruby-red radicchio with orange juice creates a deliciously dark, almost Guinness-like juice.

½ head **radicchio**
   chopped
3 **oranges**
   peeled

Juice the radicchio, then the oranges. Blend together.

■ Radicchio is a peppery Italian plant, related to red chicory. It can be the size of chicory or round like a head of Boston lettuce.

■ Radicchio adds a whopping amount of vitamin C and folic acid to the commonplace glass of orange juice. It also cleanses the blood and remineralizes the body.

Creamy crimson
beetroot | yogurt | mustard seed

Creamy crimson

Pungent

Beetroot juice is more vibrant and flavorful than its whole, cooked form. A swirl of yogurt and a dusting of mustard seeds add the finishing touches.

---

2 **beetroots**
 tops and bottoms removed
3½fl oz (100ml) **live yogurt**
1 tsp **mustard seeds**
 plus an extra pinch for
 sprinkling

Juice the beetroot. Blend with the remaining ingredients and serve with a sprinkling of mustard seeds on top.

■ *Mustard is sold as seeds, greens, oils and powders. The heat is found in black mustard seeds, thanks to the presence of myronate.*

■ *Mustard seeds increase the appetite and get the gastric juices flowing.*

Persian juice box

Spectacular

This is how my Persian friend was taught to "drink" pomegranates by his father. Pomegranates grow prolifically throughout Iran, and they would pick them off the trees on family hikes.

---

1 **pomegranate**

Press the pads of your thumbs against the skin of the pomegranate, rotating all around the fruit. This breaks the seeds inside, releasing them of their juice. When the skin is perfectly massaged, take a tiny, careful bite from a small piece of skin and suck out the delicious juice. When all the juice is gone, break open the pomegranate and pick out the seeds left intact.

■ *We call this drink aabeh doug, which, roughly translated from Farsi, the language of Iran, means "squeezable fruit."*

Three pm:

Bodies get tired, very tired, at this time of day. Resources are down. Lunchbreak is a distant memory, but the day is far from over. Voices inside cry for a little mid-afternoon fuel, quickly. When this voice is heard we have a crucial choice to make: will it be a quick fix or a long-lasting solution?

For the average juice aficionado, the choice is simple. A little liquid fruit or vegetable will raise and maintain energy levels. It will revitalize the body and clear the mind. And if lunch isn't such a distant memory, it will cleanse the palate. Junk foods and caffeine, on the other hand, will provide a quick ascent, and an even quicker descent. The choice is yours. We prefer to juice, drink and wake up.

Energizers

Coconut dream
strawberry | banana | coconut milk

Coconut dream

Lush

A strawberry and coconut lover's dream. Imagine you're on a beach on a balmy summer's afternoon.

2 handfuls **strawberries**
  hulled
1 **banana**
  peeled
2 Tbsp **coconut milk**
4 **ice cubes**

Juice the strawberries. Transfer to a blender with the banana, coconut milk and ice. Blend thoroughly. Serve topped with freshly shaved coconut if desired.

■ *Strawberries supply the super-nutrient, ellagic acid, and vitamin C. Both coat the lining of the lungs and fight free radicals.*

■ *For an even healthier alternative, 2 tablespoons of silken tofu can be substituted for the coconut milk.*

Recharger

Sun-sweetened

Dates are a high-energy food. They are the fruit of the palm tree, and in many parts of the world this is the plant on which life depends.

1 **apple**
  cored and quartered
Squeeze **lemon juice**
1 **banana**
  peeled
6 **dried dates**
  stoned
4 Tbsp **live yogurt**

Juice the apple. Transfer to a blender and add the remaining ingredients. Blend thoroughly.

■ *Dates are very high in natural sugars and provide a large amount of energy.*

■ *Ripe bananas have a naturally higher glycemic index. This means they contain sugars that are quickly absorbed for fast energy replacement.*

Royal lassi
Creamy

This super-thick blender smoothie is a take on the traditional Indian lassi.

---

1 banana
  peeled
½ mango
  peeled and stoned
6 Tbsp soy milk
  chilled
10 drops royal jelly
4 ice cubes

Put all the ingredients in a blender and blend thoroughly.

■ Royal jelly is the only food fed to the queen bee by worker bees. Because the queen bee lives much longer (3–5 years as opposed to 6–8 weeks), it is assumed that royal jelly is highly beneficial.

■ Soy milk closely resembles cow's milk in color and consistency, but it is produced entirely from the soybean.

Carrot charger
Zesty

Spirulina is an energy booster and useful post-exercise supplement. It will help speed recovery and replenish nutrient stores.

---

3 carrots
  tops and bottoms removed
1 orange
  peeled
2 tsp spirulina powder
1 tsp sesame seeds

Juice the carrots and orange. Stir in the spirulina and sesame seeds.

■ Spirulina is a form of algae which contains a wide variety of nutrients including iron, beta-carotene and vitamin B12.

■ Sesame seeds are an excellent source of linolenic acids. They also contain a lot of protein and calcium.

Carrot charger
carrot | orange | spirulina | sesame seed

Sweet red
raspberry | cranberry | lemongrass | elderflower cordial | water

Sweet red
Quenching

This drink is a fusion of flavors from around the globe.

---

2 handfuls **raspberries** (fresh/frozen)
2 handfuls **cranberries** (fresh/frozen)
½ stalk **lemongrass** trimmed and chopped
1 Tbsp **elderflower cordial**
6fl oz (175ml) **mineral water** (still or sparkling)

Juice the raspberries, cranberries and lemongrass together. Make up the elderflower cordial with the water in a tumbler. Pour the cordial over the berry juice and stir.

■ *Cranberries are often used to prevent or treat urinary tract infections.*

■ *Lemongrass is of Asian origin, and its alternative name is citronella, which is often used to repel mosquitoes.*

One
Warming

One of everything is often the case when we're juicing and the fridge is full. This is a no-fail "one" combination, regardless of ripeness or variety of fruit.

---

1 **carrot** top and bottom removed
1 **orange** peeled
1 large **apple** cored and quartered
2 tsp **roughly chopped fresh ginger**

Juice the carrot, orange and apple together. Blend with the ginger, then strain to remove any fibrous ginger bits.

■ *Ginger is a warming and soothing spice, perfect for less-than-perfect afternoons. It stimulates circulation, eases aches and pains and helps relieve colds.*

Power punch
spinach | celery | garlic | cayenne | still water

Power punch

Fiery

Make sure you wash your juicer thoroughly after making this drink. Its powerful presence will linger if you don't.

2 bunches **spinach**
   tough stalks removed
   chopped
2 stalks **celery with leaves**
   trimmed
1 **clove garlic**
   skin removed
1 pinch **cayenne**
5fl oz (150ml) **still mineral water**

Juice the spinach, celery and garlic. Stir in the cayenne and mineral water.

■ *Cayenne will help improve your circulation.*

■ *Spinach contains large amounts of the antioxidants beta-carotene and carotenoid lutein, which help maintain healthy eyes.*

Peach treat

Peachy

Peaches and strawberries are the true essence of summer fruit. Make this when they are super succulent. It's wonderful!

2 **peaches**
   stoned
1 handful **strawberries**
   hulled
1 **banana**
   peeled
1 Tbsp **flaxseed oil**
3 **ice cubes**

Juice the peaches and strawberries. Transfer to a blender and add the remaining ingredients. Blend thoroughly until the ice cubes are crushed.

■ *Flaxseed oil is the richest source of the omega-3 essential fatty acid, alpha linolenic, and can be converted in the body to the fatty acids EPA and DHA, which are those present in fish oils – perfect for non-fish eaters.*

Sweetness weakness

Refreshing

There's nothing like a glass of chilled sweetness in the afternoon to open the eyes and revive the spirit.

---

1 handful **fresh cherries**
  stoned and stalks removed
1 handful **fresh raspberries**
4 **ice cubes**

Blend all ingredients together.

■ *Both cherries and raspberries can be frozen for up to 8 months in airtight containers. If using frozen fruit, cut back on the ice cubes.*

■ *Raspberries and cherries are both rich in beta-carotene, vitamin C and calcium.*

■ *To pit cherries, cut them in half and remove the stone, or invest in a hand-held mechanical cherry-stoner. It's fiddly, but worth it.*

Pick-me-up

Tart

A sharp citrus burst for that afternoon pick-me-up.

---

2 **oranges**
  peeled
8 **mint leaves**
1 **lime**
  peeled
1 **passion fruit**
  halved and pulp scooped out

Juice the oranges, mint and lime together. Stir in the passion fruit pulp and serve with a sprig of mint.

■ *Over 100 passion fruit are needed to make 1¾pt (1L) of juice – a costly delicacy if you want to avoid the seeds.*

■ *Limes have one-and-a-half times as much acid, weight for weight, as a lemon.*

Pick-me-up
orange | mint | lime | passion fruit

Peppered orange
Crisp

Radish juice springs from the spout, looking like a strawberry milkshake. Oranges sweeten the frothy pink concoction without, thankfully, compromising its amazingly healthy, radish sensibilities.

1 bunch of **radishes**
    tops and bottoms removed
4 **oranges**
    peeled

Juice the radishes and oranges. Blend together.

■ *Radish juice is too peppery to drink alone, but it is delicious when mixed with other juices. It is extremely cleansing, clears the sinuses and stimulates the digestive system, so don't rule out radish juice.*

■ *Radishes keep well in the refrigerator. They will last longer with their leafy tops removed.*

Strawberry blond
Sweet

This juice looks spectacular when just poured, as it forms two brilliant layers of yellow and pink. Make sure you stir well before you drink to blend the flavors.

¼ **pineapple**
    peeled
1 **handful strawberries**
    hulled
1 **orange**
    peeled

Juice the pineapple and pour into a glass. Juice the strawberries and orange together and pour over the pineapple juice. Serve with a straw or spoon. Stir before drinking.

■ *Strawberries contain ellagic acid, a phytochemical that may fight cancer.*

■ *Oranges are one of the least expensive fruit sources of vitamin C.*

Strawberry blond
pineapple | strawberry | orange

Coral
apple | raspberry | strawberry | ginseng

Coral

Gentle

A lovely, gentle juice with a calming color, a delicately sweet flavor, and, with the addition of a little ginseng, an excellent source of strength and vigor.

2 **apples**
   cored and quartered
1 handful of **raspberries**
1 handful of **strawberries**
   hulled
10 drops **panax ginseng extract**

Juice the apples. Blend with the raspberries and strawberries. Stir in the ginseng extract.

■ *Raspberries and strawberries eaten out of season are often over-priced, over-sized and under-flavored. Buy them in abundance when they're fresh and freeze them in airtight freezer bags.*

■ *Ginseng helps to strengthen the body, especially when it's been under stress. It has been considered a cure-all across cultures for many generations.*

Rocket launcher

Spiked sweetness

Another energizing, slightly sweet, slightly peppery, slightly dark, slightly light – can't put your finger on it – delicious, afternoon juice. You'll love it.

1 handful of **arugula**
2 **carrots**
   tops and bottoms removed

Juice the arugula, then the carrots. Blend together.

■ *Juiced arugula, like many dark green vegetables, produces a small but concentrated juice. It adds a peppery kick to sweet juices, like carrot.*

■ *Arugula, also known as rocket, is related to watercress, mustard and radishes, which accounts for its peppery flavor.*

Tuscan nectar

Fresh

This concoction carries an earthy bottom note, a sweet middle and a tart, lemony top.

2 handfuls (approx. 30)
   seedless grapes
2 **fresh figs**
   stalks removed and halved
Juice of ½ a **lemon**

Juice the grapes, then the figs. Stir in the lemon juice.

■ Green or red grapes can be used in this recipe. Grapes produce a thick, antioxidizing juice that boosts the immune system, detoxifies the liver and clears the skin.

■ Figs are a superfood for anyone suffering from constipation, indigestion or anemia.

Kiwi

Tangy

Try and buy New Zealand "Zespri" kiwi fruit whenever possible for a superior flavor. This juice is a rich green, slightly pulpy paradise.

2 **kiwi fruits**
   peeled and halved
2 **apples**
   cored and quartered
6 **dandelion leaves**

Juice all the ingredients together.

■ Apples have a low glycemic index and keep hunger pangs at bay for longer than many other fruits.

■ Kiwi fruit contain antinidin, an enzyme which aids digestion.

Tuscan nectar

grape | fig | lemon

Goggles
carrot | celery | fennel

Goggles
Salty licorice

A slightly savory, cleansing drink to perk up your afternoon, improve vision and prepare you for the night ahead…

1 **carrot**
  top and bottom removed, chopped
2 stalks **celery**
  chopped
1 small **fennel bulb**
  halved and leafy tops removed

Juice the carrot, celery and fennel together. Stir.

■ *Fennel juice is vibrant in flavor and aroma. It is a wonderful cleanser and diuretic, so drink this juice in a strategic location.*

■ *Celery has a naturally salty taste, which adds life to many vegetable juices.*

Kick
Pungent

A dollop of horseradish provides a fantastic kick to this rich, energizing blend of sweetness.

2 **beetroots**
  tops and bottoms removed
2 **carrots**
  tops and bottoms removed
½ tsp **creamed horseradish**

Juice the beetroots and carrots separately. Mix the juices together and stir in the horse-radish, more or less to taste.

■ *Horseradish has a thick, hotly pungent root that resembles a parsnip. Beneath its rough skin is a white, smooth inside which contains an essential oil similar to mustard, hence the heat.*

■ *English sailors used to eat horseradish at sea to prevent scurvy. Smart, considering horseradish has more vitamin C than oranges.*

Sweet fortification
nectarine | peach | strawberry | echinacea

Sweet fortification
Fresh

Drinking this juice makes you wonder how anyone can buy store-bought concoctions.

2 **nectarines**
  halved and stoned
1 **peach**
  halved and stoned
5 **strawberries**
  hulled
5 drops **echinacea extract**

Juice the nectarines and peach together. Blend with the strawberries and echinacea.

■ *Echinacea helps boost a sluggish immune system and wards off potential colds and flu. It is most effective taken when the first, niggling signs of sickness are sensed in the body.*

■ *Peaches and nectarines are extremely perishable so are often harvested when still firm. Look for fruits that are not too hard. The harder the fruit, the less likely they are to ripen properly.*

Feijoa frenzy
Creamy

The smell and taste of feijoas, eaten straight from the tree, reminds me vividly of my childhood. Juicing them is a whole new world well worth discovering.

2 **feijoas**
  peeled
1 **apple**
  cored and quartered
4 **guavas**
  peeled
Squeeze **lemon juice**

Juice the feijoas, apple and guavas together. Add a squeeze of lemon.

■ *Feijoas grow most abundantly in New Zealand and are a good source of vitamin C.*

■ *Guavas are an excellent source of soluble fiber.*

Five pm:

Good-bye day, hello night. This is that special time when your glass of juice sheds all conservatism and slips into a pair of heels. Bring out the crystal glasses, the martini shakers and the tumblers. It's cocktail hour, and you've got a juicer.

The following recipes are our favorite non-alcoholic cocktails. No, a cocktail without alcohol is not an oxymoron. The word "cocktail" means a mélange of beverages. These days this mélange invariably includes booze. It's no surprise; alcohol makes us feel good by sedating a part of the brain that keeps our behavior in check. But who needs sedation when plump lychees are blended with grenadine and mint? Or what about a tumbler of passion fruit suspended in a bath of frothy peach? We prefer to have all faculties fully functioning at these moments. Alcohol, of course, can be added to each and every one of these drinks if sedation is required. But a word of warning: booze is kryptonite. It cripples the nutritional superpowers found in fresh juice, rendering it less beneficial.

Malibu cooler
pineapple | almond | coconut milk

Malibu cooler

Nutty

This drink will transport you to the Caribbean in seconds.

½ **pineapple**
  peeled
1 Tbsp **ground almonds**
2 Tbsp **coconut milk**
3 **ice cubes**

Juice the pineapple. Stir in the almonds and coconut milk. Pour over ice.

■ Pineapple contains bromelain, an enzyme which helps balance the body's levels of acid and alkaline and aids digestion.

■ Almonds are a good source of antioxidants, vitamin E and selenium.

Sweet sensation

Sweet

Blood oranges are much sweeter than ordinary oranges and give this drink a perfect sweet and sour balance. If blood oranges are not available use Sweet Navel or Valencia oranges instead.

½ **pineapple**
  peeled
1 **lemon**
  peeled
1 **blood orange**
  peeled

Juice all the ingredients together.

■ Bromelain, an enzyme found in pineapple, has anti-inflammatory properties and helps reduce the inflammation that results from arthritis and rheumatism.

■ Blood oranges originated by accident. The original mutation probably arose in the seventeenth century in Sicily where they are still predominantly grown today.

Grape spritzer
white grape | elderflower cordial | sparkling water

Grape spritzer

Floral

A thirst-quenching, subtly scented spritzer to add sophistication to your evening.

1 bunch **white grapes**
   stalks removed
1 tsp **elderflower cordial**
6fl oz (175ml) **sparkling mineral water**
3 **ice cubes**

Juice the grapes. Add the elderflower cordial and water. Pour over ice.

■ *Grapes are beneficial for cleansing the system.*

■ *Elderflower is useful for treating coughs, colds and sore throats.*

Pretty in pink

Crisp

A perfectly refreshing, cleansing and crisp concoction.

1 **lemon**
   peeled
1 bunch **red grapes**
   stalks removed
1 **apple**
   cored and quartered

Juice all the ingredients together. Serve over ice if desired and with a slice of lemon.

■ *Red grape varieties contain powerful polyphenols, the same as those in red wine. These are antioxidants and have a positive effect in helping to reduce the risk of heart disease.*

■ *Apples vary considerably and can be catergorized into "cooking" and "eating" apples. Both varieties are suitable for juicing.*

Cherry berry

Effervescent

Blending rather than juicing the berries creates the best results in this spectacular cocktail.

2 handfuls **raspberries**
1 handful **strawberries**
  hulled
3 handfuls **cherries**
  stoned and stalks removed
6fl oz (175ml) **cold, sparkling mineral water**

Blend the raspberries, strawberries and cherries together. Pour into a glass. Top with cold, sparkling mineral water and watch it fizz. Stir and serve immediately.

■ *Buy a year's supply of cherries while in season and freeze in airtight containers or freezer bags. They can be stored for up to a year.*

■ *The raspberry is closely related to the blackberry, but the absence of a core in the picked fruit makes raspberries softer and juicier.*

Passionate peach

Crunchy

This cocktail is delicious. The contrast between smooth and crunch is a palate pleaser.

2 **peaches**
  halved and stoned
8 **mint leaves**
  chopped
2 **passion fruit**
  halved and pulp scooped out
4 **ice cubes**

Juice the peach and mint together. Add the passion fruit pulp and pour over ice. Serve with a sprig of mint.

■ *Passion fruit has so much perfume and so little pulp – much like a precious vanilla pod.*

■ *There are about two dozen species of mint and many hundreds of varieties. All are very different in flavor and aroma.*

Passionate peach
peach | mint | passion fruit

Blue spice

Spicy

A dark, moody juice for the most sophisticated of cocktail parties.

---

1 **orange**
   peeled
3 handfuls **blueberries**
1 **apple**
   cored and quartered
2 pinches **ground nutmeg**
1 pinch **ground cinnamon**

Juice the orange, blueberries and apple. Stir in the nutmeg and cinnamon.

■ *Nutmeg is hallucinogenic when consumed in excess, but a little pinch included in a drink is a useful relaxer.*

■ *Blueberries contain anthocyanosides; antibacterial pigments which have a beneficial effect on blood vessels and the treatment of varicose veins.*

Blue spice
orange | blueberry | apple
nutmeg | cinnamon

Virgin mary

Peppery

This juice is a non-alcoholic version of a Bloody Mary.

1 large **tomato**
   halved
2 stalks **celery**
   trimmed and chopped
Splash **Worcestershire sauce**
Pinch **sea salt**
Pinch **black pepper**
1 leafy stalk **celery**
   to garnish

Juice the tomato, then the celery. Stir together and add remaining ingredients. Top with a leafy stalk of celery and serve immediately, before the tomato juice separates.

■ *Sea salt is flaky, crystal salt which is made by panning sea salts. It has a pronounced salty taste, meaning less is more!*

■ *Worcestershire sauce is a blend of malt vinegar, molasses, anchovies, tamarind, onions, garlic and spices. It adds zing to vegetable juices.*

Quenching heat

Piquant

This cocktail is inspired by Mexican popsicles, which are often a blend of fruit juice and hot chilies. The sweet green flesh of the honeydew melon partners perfectly with chilies – a simultaneously sweet, exhilarating and refreshing drink.

¼ **honeydew melon**
   peeled and chopped
2–3 **ice cubes**
½ tsp **dried chili pepper**

Juice the melon. Blend with ice cubes, then stir in the chili pepper.

■ *Honeydew melon is a winter melon. Winter melons are slightly oblong in shape and have a longer shelf-life. Honeydew melon has smooth, yellow skin and sweet, green flesh.*

■ *Chili pepper is the perfect cure-all; it aids in digestion, stimulates circulation, kills bacteria, clears congestion, prevents ulcers and relieves pain.*

Mango lush
mango | lemongrass | ginger | apple

Mango lush

Tropical

Make sure you choose a firm but ripe mango for this juice. Underripe mangoes have a slightly astringent taste.

1 **mango**
   peeled and stoned
½ stalk **lemongrass**
   trimmed and chopped
⅕in (0.5cm) piece **fresh ginger**
   peeled
1 **apple**
   cored and quartered

Juice all the ingredients together.

■ *Mangoes are a seasonal fruit, but they can be frozen. Peel and stone the fruit and store in freezer bags or an air-tight container. This means that you'll have them on hand at all times.*

■ *You could use a little lemongrass powder if fresh is not available, but the flavor won't be as intense.*

Fruit soother

Warming

A hot-toddy-inspired pre-dinner drink to warm the body and soothe the soul.

½ **lime**
   peeled
5 **strawberries**
   hulled
4fl oz (25ml) **boiling water**
1 Tbsp **elderberry cordial**

Juice the lime, then blend with the strawberries. Stir in boiling water and the elderberry cordial and serve immediately.

■ *Elderberry cordial is an unfermented, non-alcoholic concentrate.*

■ *The elderberry tree, which grows all over Europe, parts of Asia and North America, bears white flowers and black berries which are both edible.*

Raspberry zinger
raspberry | lime | orange | mint

Raspberry zinger

Sharp

A refreshing and zingy cocktail to get the party started. A frosted glass, an icy-pink blend and a sprinkling of mint – what could be better?

3 handfuls **raspberries**
1 **lime**
   peeled
2 **oranges**
   peeled
6 **mint leaves**
3 **ice cubes**

Juice the raspberries, lime and oranges together. Chop the mint finely and combine. Pour over ice cubes.

■ *Raspberries can range in color from white through yellow, orange, pink, red and purple to black.*

■ *Did you know that there is such a thing as sweet limes? They originated in the Middle East and India and are almost completely devoid of acidity.*

Ginger sweet

Tart

Lemonade dressed up with a touch of ginger and a dash of bubbles.

1 **lemon**
   peeled
1 Tbsp **stem ginger**
   chopped
1 tsp **stem ginger syrup**
8fl oz (250ml) **sparkling mineral water**
Lemon wedges

Juice the lemon. Blend with the stem ginger and strain. Add syrup. Top with sparkling water and lemon wedges.

■ *Lemons are rich in calcium, chlorine, magnesium, phosphorus, sodium and sulphur.*

■ *Sparkling mineral water is water naturally charged with carbon dioxide. Carbonated water is an eighteenth century invention designed to emulate the real thing.*

Holiday

Tropical

This cool, thick concoction will transport you to the beach, pronto.

½ **pineapple**
   peeled
2 Tbsp **coconut milk**
1 **banana**
   peeled
2–3 **ice cubes**

Juice the pineapple. Blend with coconut milk, banana and ice.

■ *There are four main varieties of pineapple: Cayenne, Queen, Red Spanish, Pernambuco.*

■ *Choose a pineapple that is heavy for its size and aromatic. If it smells particularly strongly, it's probably overripe.*

Fusion

Aromatic

The Middle East meets cooler climes with this delicately sweet, pink cocktail.

6 **plums**
   halved and stoned
½ **lime**
   peeled
½ **pomegranate**
   seeds removed from skin

Juice the plums and lime. Blend pomegranate seeds and strain. Blend with the juice.

■ *Sweet, aromatic plum juice goes well with any berry juice. Choose plums that are firm but ripe.*

■ *Lime juice cuts the sweetness, without lending too much tartness to the drink.*

Rosé

Sweet

This elegant drink has a wonderfully delicate, sweet flavor.

---

1 **peach**
  halved and stoned
¼ **watermelon**
  flesh scooped out
6 **mint leaves**
1 splash **rosewater**
3 **ice cubes**

Juice the peach, watermelon and mint together. Add a splash of rosewater and pour over ice. Serve immediately with a sprig of mint and rose petals on top.

■ *Rosewater is the natural essence of roses – simply scented water made with rose petals.*

■ *There is no need to remove the seeds from the watermelon before juicing. The Chinese are even particularly fond of eating them.*

Rosé
peach | watermelon
mint | rosewater

Pearly red

Floral

A blend where canned lychees are allowed and frozen cranberries are just fine – the perfect off-the-shelf cocktail.

---

1 handful **cranberries**
8 **lychees**
  peeled
2–3 **ice cubes**

Juice the cranberries. Blend with lychees and ice.

■ *A lychee is a small, round fruit with a thin, reddish shell and a pearly white, edible middle. Its flavor is similar to a rose, a strawberry and a Muscat grape.*

■ *Lychees are sensitive to cold temperatures and are very perishable – hence the need for a canned lychee once in a while.*

Heaven scent

Silky

"That is the magic of floral smells...when you taste them, the flavor still eludes you, as if you are eating a piece of a place that might not exist, or a memory of something that never really happened..."
Diana Henry, *Crazy Water Pickled Lemons*.

---

8 **lychees**
  peeled
1 tsp **rosewater**
2–3 **ice cubes**
1 tsp **grenadine**

Blend the lychees with the rosewater and ice. Pour in grenadine.

■ *Grenadine is a sweet, deep red, pomegranate-flavored syrup used to color and flavor drinks and desserts. Originally, grenadine was made from pomegranates grown on the island of Grenada in the Caribbean. Now other fruit-juice concentrates are also used to make the syrup.*

Heaven scent
lychee | rosewater | grenadine

Strawberry must
strawberry | balsamic vinegar | cream | honey

Strawberry must

Indulgent

Brows may furrow as you deftly splash balsamic vinegar into the tumbler; little do they know you're serving decadence in a glass.

2 handfuls **strawberries**
  hulled
2 tsp **balsamic vinegar**
3fl oz (75ml) **cream**
Honey
  to taste
1–2 **ice cubes**

Blend the strawberries. Pour in the balsamic vinegar, cream and honey to taste. Serve over ice.

■ *True balsamic vinegar comes from Modena and Reggio in Italy. Buy the most expensive balsamic vinegar that you can afford and use it sparingly.*

■ *Cream is the thick layer that rises to the top of unhomogenized milk. It's generally a no-no in any health-conscious diet, but come on, everything in moderation, right?*

Cydonia

Smooth

A quince looks like a mutated apple, or is it a mutated pear? Either way, its juice is a beautiful mélange of both and pairs well with a bevy of juices.

1 **peach**
  halved and stoned
1 **quince**
  peeled and deseeded
¼ **watermelon**
  flesh scooped out

Juice the peach, quince and watermelon. Stir to combine.

■ *If a quince isn't at hand, substitute a large pear or large apple.*

■ *Quinces were cultivated in the Levant and southeast Europe long before the apple. It has had many names over the past 2,000 or so years; the Greeks called it* cydonia; *to the Romans it was* melimelum, *loosely translated as "honey apple," which indicates its future as a fruit destined for use in preserves.*

Nine pm:

Some say it's best to end with the beginning. So take out your juicer, blender, citrus press and kettle one last time and make yourself an evening elixir. The concoction you create could be a comforting drink filled with favorite tastes from familiar times – it might be lavender-infused milk or a blend of chamomile and ginger to lull you to sleep. If it's a stomach soother you're after, perhaps it will be a splash of fennel with a hint of ginger. But then again, not everyone wants to fall asleep straight away. That's where the seductive powers of nutmeg and vanilla come into play. Regardless of what you're in the mood for this evening, there's a drink for you. However, before you take a sip, fill the sink with hot water, put on your rubber gloves and lovingly wash your juicer, blender, pot, whisk. Seize this moment, because nothing is worse than dried pulp in the morning.

Blackberry pie

blackberry | apple | cinnamon

Blackberry pie

Spicy

We love blackberry and apple pie. By warming this drink you can almost imagine you are eating it. Let your imagination go wild and you might even be able to taste the vanilla ice cream, too.

2 handfuls **blackberries**
2 **apples**
   cored and quartered
1 pinch **ground cinnamon**

Juice the blackberries and apples together. Stir in the cinnamon. Serve cool, or warm it over a moderate heat.

■ *Blackberries and apples contain pectin, a soluble fiber which helps eliminate cholesterol and protects against environmental toxins.*

■ *Cinnamon is often used as an antidote for diarrhea and stomach upsets.*

Aromatic soother

Autumnal

Make sure you choose firm, but ripe pears. Unripe pears produce an astringent-tasting juice. A perfectly selected pear will make a sweet, soothing drink.

2 **pears**
   cored and quartered
1 pinch **ground ginger**
1 Tbsp **honey**
4 Tbsp **live yogurt**
1 pinch **ground nutmeg**

Juice the pears. Stir in the remaining ingredients and sprinkle the nutmeg on top.

■ *Ripe pears are said to be sedative. Make sure you choose your pears well and you will sleep like a baby.*

■ *Nutmeg is an aphrodisiac, so watch your balance of nutmeg and pear.*

Pine melon

Zingy

Watermelon leaves a very wet pulp behind – be extra careful when cleaning up not to spill it everywhere.

¼ **watermelon**
   flesh and seeds scooped out
¼ **pineapple**
   peeled
⅕in (0.5cm) piece **fresh ginger**
   skin removed

Juice the watermelon, pineapple and ginger together.

■ *Pineapple contains the enzyme bromelain. This aids digestion for a better sleep.*

■ *Watermelon is quite distinct in flavor and color from ordinary sweet melons. It also contains a good amount of beta-carotene.*

Tomato tonic

Garlicky

If you're a fan of tomato juice you'll love this one – sweet, hot and herby all in one.

4 **tomatoes**
   stalks removed
1 **clove garlic**
   peeled
6 **sage leaves**
1 Tbsp **runny honey**
3 **ice cubes**

Juice the tomatoes, garlic and sage together. Stir in the honey thoroughly and pour over ice.

■ *Garlic is most beneficial in its raw state, before the protective, volatile compounds have been destroyed.*

■ *Sage is a calming herb and will help induce sleep.*

Tomato tonic
tomato I garlic I sage I honey

Floo fighter

Sharp

Fight away any potential colds with this calming, high-in-vitamin-C drink. This can also be made using hot, instead of chilled, tea.

2 **lemons**
  peeled
⅓in (1cm) **piece fresh ginger**
  peeled
7fl oz (200ml) **chamomile tea**
  chilled

Juice the lemons and ginger together. Add the chamomile tea and stir.

■ *Chamomile is a diuretic, so try not to consume this drink too close to bedtime.*

■ *Lemons contain linolene, which helps ward off cancer.*

Floo fighter
lemon I ginger
chamomile tea

Fig fix

Vanilla

A highly fragrant, delicious smoothie for fig and vanilla lovers – a perfect bedtime pleasure.

1 **orange**
  peeled
2 **fresh figs**
  stems removed and halved
1 **vanilla pod**
  seeds scooped out
6 Tbsp **live yogurt**
2 tsp **honey**

Juice the orange. Transfer to a blender and blend with the remaining ingredients. (Use only the vanilla seeds. Discard the pod or put it into a container filled with castor sugar to add a vanilla flavor to your baking.)

■ *Vanilla has aphrodisiac properties. It is often used as a perfume to seduce.*

■ *Figs are beneficial if suffering from indigestion after a large meal.*

Fig fix
orange | fig
vanilla | yogurt | honey

Maple marvel
plum | cinnamon | yogurt | maple syrup

Maple marvel
Sweet

Maple syrup is made from the sap of the maple tree. It gives this drink its distinctive sweetness and a Canadian twist.

3 **plums**
   halved and stoned
2 pinches **ground cinnamon**
6 Tbsp **live yogurt**
2 Tbsp **maple syrup**

Juice the plums. Stir in the remaining ingredients and mix thoroughly.

■ *Maple syrup contains fewer calories and more minerals than honey.*

■ *Plums are a good source of fiber. Choose red-skinned varieties, as they contain useful amounts of beta-carotene.*

Soy content
Frothy

Soy milk is much gentler on the stomach than cow's milk, making this the perfect, vitamin-rich, evening soother.

2 **fresh figs**
   stalk removed and halved
4 **oranges**
   peeled
3 Tbsp **soy milk**
1 tsp **runny honey**

Juice the figs and oranges together. Stir in soy milk and honey.

■ *Figs contain a protedytic enzyme that is considered an aid to digestion.*

■ *Soy milk has a characteristic taste that can take some getting used to, but blending it with fruit juices masks its distinct flavor.*

Clean living

Aniseed

Fennel to soothe, carrot to sweeten and parsley to restore whatever was lost throughout the day and provide stamina for the night.

½ **fennel bulb**
  outer part removed
2 **carrots**
  tops and bottoms removed, chopped
2 heaped Tbsp **parsley**

Juice the fennel and carrots. Blend with parsley.

■ *Parsley is loaded with vitamins, especially A and C, and is rich in riboflavin, calcium, iron, magnesium and potassium.*

■ *Fennel soothes the stomach and aids in digestion.*

Pacific perfection

Lush

The right selection of Pacific island fruits make for the perfect evening relaxer.

¼ **pineapple**
  peeled
½ **mango**
  peeled and stoned
2 **passion fruits**
  flesh scooped out

Juice the pineapple and mango. Stir in the passion fruit.

■ *People double their need for vitamins when in a stressed state. This juice will help you relax, unwind and de-stress.*

■ *Mangoes are one of the few good fruit sources of vitamin E.*

Pacific perfection

pineapple | mango | passion fruit

Sage citrus

Herby

In medieval times sage was thought to be medicinal. It had a reputation for having restorative powers. This may still be true today.

2 **oranges**
  peeled
1 **lemon**
  peeled
6 **sage leaves**
4 **ice cubes**

Juice the oranges, lemon and sage together. Pour over ice.

■ *Sage is a calming herb and has also been shown to reduce hot flashes during menopause.*

■ *Citrus fruits collectively constitute the third most popular group of fruits; only apples and pears and bananas and plantains surpass them in quantity produced and consumed.*

Sage citrus
orange | lemon
sage

Crocus milk

Aromatic

Saffron's distinctive, yellowy hue and aromatic flavor lend a special touch to creamy bananas and milk.

Pinch **saffron**
    soaked in 1 tsp hot water
1 **banana**
    peeled
4fl oz (125ml) **whole milk**

Blend ingredients together.

■ *Saffron aids in digestion and relieves flatulence.*

■ *Whole milk contains approximately 3.5% fat, while low fat or skimmed milk contains 1–2% fat. The latter, however, doesn't have the same decadent richness as the former.*

Crocus milk
saffron
banana | milk

Aroma therapy
Aromatic

Lavender, blended with gifts from the land of milk and honey, will calm, soothe and lull you to sleep.

8fl oz (250ml) **whole milk**
1 tsp **honey**
1 tsp **lavender seeds**

In a saucepan, over a low heat, gently warm the milk, honey and lavender. Strain.

■ *The word lavender comes from the Latin word* lavare, *meaning "wash"; hence its popularity as a fragrance for soaps, shampoos and sachets. But lavender is also a natural remedy, helping relieve insomnia, anxiety, depression and mood swings.*

■ *Deer hate lavender's strong smell. Bushes of lavender throughout the garden will protect your roses from deer – that is, if you're lucky enough to have roses, or deer, for that matter.*

Perfect pair
Ethereal

A beautiful couple, pears and pine nuts, juiced into one harmonious blend.

2 **pears**
   halved and cored
1 Tbsp **pine nuts**
   toasted

Juice the pears. Blend with toasted pine nuts.

■ *Toasting pine nuts, or any nuts for that matter, before using them in a recipe will heighten their flavor. Toast in a hot pan or briefly under the grill.*

■ *Pine nuts, borne on the scales of pinecones, are produced by several varieties of pine trees. Most varieties are found in southern Europe, mainly Italy and France. A large cone can bear up to 100 seeds.*

Perfect pair
pear | pine nuts

Orange blossom
apricot | peach | orange flower water

Orange blossom

Fragrant

This fruit juice has a real Middle Eastern twist. Orange flower water is prominent in these countries and is sometimes even added to flavor Turkish coffee. Turkey is also one of the main regions of apricot cultivation.

2 **apricots**
   halved and stoned
2 **peaches**
   halved and stoned
1 splash **orange flower water**

Juice the apricots and peaches together. Add a splash of orange flower water and stir.

■ *Orange flower water is sometimes called orange blossom water. It is the product of the distillation of orange flowers from the bitter orange. It can be added to water, with sugar, as a soothing bedtime drink.*

■ *Apricots are one of the best natural sources of vitamin A, which is essential for healthy skin and mucous membranes.*

Prunus domestica

Gentle

A thick, mildly sweet, bedtime treat.

2 **plums**
   halved and stoned
1 **banana**
   peeled
7fl oz (200ml) **soy milk**

Juice the plums. Blend with the banana and soy milk.

■ *Plums are best in late summer, fresh from the tree. When plums are not in season, substitute summer or winter melons.*

■ *Plums range in color from crimson to purple to greenish-yellow. The Damson plum is a blue-skinned variety with a tart flavor that subsides with a squirt of honey.*

Tender tummy
Licorice

Fennel and ginger soothe the stomach like nothing else. But beware – fennel juice is amazingly potent. Add slowly until the perfect aniseed equilibrium is reached.

½ **fennel**
  outer part removed
2 **apples**
  halved and cored
1 pinch **ground ginger**

Juice the fennel and apples separately. Add fennel juice to apple juice to taste. Sprinkle ginger on top. Stir.

■ *Fennel, also known as Florence fennel, resembles a squat, thick head of celery, but its distinctive licorice flavor sets it apart.*

■ *Fennel soothes acidic stomachs, flatulence, stomachache and nausea. It is an excellent source of potassium and contains vitamin C, folic acid, magnesium and phosphorus.*

Tender tummy
fennel | apple
ginger

Citrus city

Tart

Can't decide which citrus fruits to juice? No worries; juice them all.

---

1 **grapefruit**
  peeled
1 **orange**
  peeled
Juice of ½ **lemon**
Juice of ½ **lime**

Juice the grapefruit, orange, lemon and lime. Stir.

■ *The pith – found between the flesh and skin of citrus fruits – contains pectin and bioflavinoids, which add copious antioxidants to the mix.*

■ *Most citrus fruits are juiceable, except Seville oranges. They are best used in sauces, stews and marmalades.*

Citrus city
grapefruit | orange
lemon | lime

Convalescent
grape | papaya | lemon

Convalescent

Sweet

A drink so deliciously soothing it makes washing your juicer worth it every time.

---

2 handfuls **grapes**
1 **papaya**
   peeled and seeds
   scooped out
Juice of ½ **lemon**

Juice the grapes, papaya and lemon. Stir.

■ *Papaya juice is a favorite of Anna Selby, author of* The Juice and Zest Book. *Take heed: Selby warns that the skin and seeds can cause itching, so wash your hands well – invaluable advice.*

■ *Grapes are rich in calcium, magnesium, phosphorus, flavonoids, potassium and vitamins C and E. Grape juice is very sweet, and remember, the riper the grape, the sweeter the juice.*

Pear and ginger quencher

Crisp

Iced teas are making a revival. Combined with freshly squeezed fruit juice this infused iced tea is thirst-quenching and delicious.

---

1 Tbsp **stem ginger syrup**
1 stalk **lemongrass**
1 **green tea bag**
1 **lemon**
   peeled
1 **pear**
   cored and quartered
Ice

Place the ginger syrup, lemongrass and tea bag in a heatproof bowl. Add 5fl oz (150ml) boiling water. Remove the tea bag after 3–4 minutes. Juice the lemon and pear and add to the infused tea mixture. Serve warm or over ice.

■ *Lemongrass relaxes the stomach and relieves cramp and flatulence.*

Cleansers

Everyday life drains the goodness from our bodies, regardless of how healthy we are. We cannot escape the environment in which we live, but we can control what we eat. Fresh juices are easily absorbed by the body, making them the fastest way to restore our vitamin and mineral reserves. And not only do they restore, juices can also spring clean as they go, reaching the innermost parts of our body that we rarely even think about.

The following recipes feature fruits and vegetables known for their spectacular cleansing powers. We prefer to call them cleansers rather than detoxers, mainly because the word "detox," along with "natural" and "organic," are so often misused. Detoxing your body – whether just for a day, a week or a fortnight – is the best present you could ever give yourself. However, in order to do it safely and properly, it's best to consult a healthcare professional beforehand.

Magenta miracle
Pulpy

It takes a while to get used to the pulpy texture and unusual taste of this drink. Don't drink too much in one sitting or you may encounter some rather anti-social consequences.

1 **baby red cabbage**
   outer leaves removed
¼ **head iceberg lettuce**
   outer leaves removed

Juice both ingredients together.

■ *Cabbage contains sulphur compounds that clear out toxins and also have an antioxidant effect.*

■ *The lettuce belongs to the very large family* Compositae, *which includes cultivated species such as chicory and various wild plants with edible leaves, e.g. dandelion leaves.*

Magenta miracle
red cabbage
iceberg lettuce

Berrylicious

Sharp

This juice is an antioxidant, immune system-boosting, cleansing tonic. What more could you want?

1 handful **strawberries** hulled
2 handfuls **raspberries**
2 handfuls **wheatgrass** rinsed and chopped
4 **ice cubes**

Juice the strawberries, raspberries and wheatgrass together. Transfer to a blender and blend with the ice.

■ *Raspberries are one of the best fruit sources of fiber.*

■ *Strawberries are an excellent source of vitamin C. There is approximately twice the daily recommended nutrient intake (RNI) for adults (77mg) in one handful.*

Berrylicious
strawberry | raspberry
wheatgrass

Waterfall

Sweet

One of our most simple juices and, as far as we're concerned, one of our best.

¼ **watermelon**
　flesh and seeds scooped out
1 **lime**
　peeled

Juice the watermelon and lime together.

■ *Watermelon contains lycopene and beta-carotene and is an excellent cleanser. The seeds are extremely nutritious too, containing a plentiful supply of minerals such as zinc and selenium.*

■ *Consumed first thing in the morning (on an empty stomach) fruit acids are effective detoxifiers.*

Waterfall
watermelon
lime

Ginger glory

Hot

This simple concoction of pear, grape and ginger is worth its weight in gold. Try it; you'll be surprised how delicious it is.

---

2 **pears**
   cored and quartered
¾in (2cm) piece **fresh ginger**
   peeled
1 bunch **white grapes**
   stalks removed

Juice the pears, ginger and grapes.

■ *Ginger contains powerful, volatile oils – zingiberene and gingero – which act as gentle cleansers.*

■ *Grapes have a laxative effect and are useful if suffering from constipation.*

Ginger glory
pear | ginger
grape

Red
chicory | carrot | red pepper

Red

Bite

This trio of goodness will cleanse your system, energize your body and improve your eyesight simultaneously.

1 head **chicory**
1 **carrot**
   top and bottom removed
   chopped
1 **red pepper**
   stem removed, deseeded
   chopped

Juice chicory, carrot and red pepper together. Stir.

■ *Chicory is an excellent liver and blood cleanser and contains quantities of beta-carotene which strengthens vision. It produces a bitter juice, however, so always mix it with other vegetable juices.*

■ *Red pepper juice is surprisingly mild. It stimulates circulation and digestion, essential for the cleansing process.*

Prickly Heat

Pungent

If your liver requires a little bit of tender loving care, then this is the drink for you.

3 **beetroot with leaves**
1 **apple**
   cored and quartered
1 pinch **cayenne**
5 drops **milk thistle extract**

Juice the beetroot and the apple together. Stir in the cayenne and milk thistle extract.

■ *Milk thistle helps protect and strengthen liver cells. It is useful in cases of jaundice, hepatitis and alcohol abuse.*

■ *Cayenne is a highly pungent spice made from the ground seeds of the chili pepper.*

Clean
Creamy

A clean, creamy cleanser with a hint of sweetness and a sprinkling of mint.

¼ (7oz/200g) **cucumber**
  chopped
1 **apple**
  cored and chopped
4 **mint leaves**

Juice cucumber, apple and mint. Stir.

■ *Cucumbers are one of the best vegetable cleansers. They have both diuretic and laxative properties and improve skin, hair and nails.*

■ *Even a small piece of cucumber adds an almost dairy-like thickness to juices – perfect if you love dairy, but dairy doesn't love you.*

Clean
cucumber | apple
mint

Green day

Clean

These savory greens will flow through the system and take unwanted baggage with them.

¼ (7oz/200g) **cucumber** chopped
Small handful **parsley**
Small handful **alfalfa sprouts**

Juice cucumber. Blend with parsley and sprouts.

■ *Alfalfa sprouts are practically complete in nutritive value. They're high in vitamins, minerals and proteins.*

■ *To grow alfalfa sprouts: put 1 tablespoon of dry seeds into a glass jar. Soak seeds in water overnight; strain, rinse and put in a clean glass jar with a wide mouth. Cover with muslin and secure with a metal ring or elastic band. Turn the jar over and put in a warm, dark place. Rinse the seeds twice daily for 3–4 days; strain and return jar to same location for 3–4 days. Don't let the seeds dry out. When sprouts are 1–2in (2.5–5cm) long, expose them to sunlight for a day to allow the leaves to turn green.*

Green day
cucumber | parsley
alfalfa sprouts

Royal flush

Potent

If this juice doesn't make you feel cleansed, nothing will. For maximum cleansing effect, drink this concoction in the morning, several times a week.

1 **beetroot with leaves**
1 **carrot**
   top and bottom removed, chopped
1 **apple**
   cored and chopped
¾in (2cm) piece **fresh ginger**
   peeled
Juice of ½ **lime**
   peeled

Juice beetroot, carrot, apple, ginger and lime. Stir.

■ *Carrot juice is the queen of all vegetable juices. Besides being a potent antioxidant, protector against cancer and infections, it cleanses the liver, kidneys and entire digestive tract. Too much carrot juice will turn you orange, literally, so take it easy and mix it with other juices.*

Royal flush
beetroot | carrot
apple | ginger | lime

Inner cleanse
Lush

When things don't seem to be moving quite as they should, try this papaya pleasure and you'll be on your way soon.

1 **papaya**
seeds discarded (or use if your prefer) and flesh scooped out
⅓in (1cm) piece **fresh ginger**
peeled
1 **pear**
cored and quartered
Squeeze of **lemon juice**

Juice the papaya, ginger and pear together. Stir in the lemon juice.

■ *There are over 3,000 known pear varieties in the world. However, only a few are grown for commercial production.*

■ *The seeds of the papaya are edible and have a spicy flavor – somewhat reminiscent of black pepper.*

Citrus froth
Tart

A sweet, red juice topped with crisp, bubbly foam – medicinal sophistication at its best.

1 **grapefruit**
peeled
2 **blood oranges**
peeled
¼ **cucumber**
chopped

Juice the grapefruit, oranges and cucumber together. Stir.

■ *This juice will vary in redness, depending on the variety of the blood orange used.*

■ *It's a mystery as to why the cucumber gives this juice a frothy, cappuccino-like consistency, but it's the mystery that makes this juice so magical.*

Juicy ingredients

Every ingredient used in the juices in this book brings a history, a taste, a texture and a health-giving property to the table. Exercising creativity with ingredients is exciting. Understanding why juices are beneficial is the challenge. This chapter is designed to help you with this. Just as we ask doctors for complete information on our healthcare options, we should also find out as much as we can about the foods we put into our bodies. Where do they come from? How are they grown? How should they be purchased and prepared? Why do our bodies need them?

Many of the juices in this book include herbal remedies. The concept of using herbs as medicine is hardly new. The Chinese have been following this practice for thousands of years. However, self-healing with herbs is a relatively new concept in the Western world. They provide the body with innumerable benefits. When shopping for such ingredients, don't be afraid to inquire about particular remedies, recommended doses, benefits and origins of ingredients.

Fruits and vegetables

Ingredient	Seasonality	Storage tips/juicing preparation
Alfalfa sprouts	Alfalfa is germinated indoors so it can be purchased or grown at home at any time of year. When buying sprouted seeds, look for firm sprouts with small, green, fresh-smelling leaves.	Can be bought sprouted or in seed form. Buy a small amount of seeds – a little goes a long way. Once sprouted, alfalfa can be kept in the refrigerator for up to 1 week.
Apple	Myriad varieties are available throughout the year, but are best when purchased locally from late summer through early winter.	Store in a cool, dry place. The flesh oxidizes quickly when exposed to air. Drink quickly to avoid murky juice, or add a little lime or lemon juice to keep the color. Pull out the stems and core before juicing.
Apricot	Fresh apricots are a summer fruit; Italy and Turkey are the biggest exporters.	Apricots spoil quickly when bruised. Store in a cool dry place.
Arugula (rocket)	Arugula is particularly plentiful in late summer. Look for bright green leaves that are delicately crisp.	Place unwashed arugula in a plastic bag, closing it loosely to admit some air, and refrigerate.
Avocado	A spring fruit grown in warm climates – USA, Central and South America.	Leave to ripen at room temperature. Sprinkle flesh with lemon juice to prevent discoloration.

Benefits	Approximate juice yield	Ingredient
Sprouted seeds contain folic acid and zinc. They are a diuretic and stimulant and alleviate scurvy, peptic ulcers and urinary problems.	Best when blended, not juiced. One ⅓oz (10g) bunch yields approximately 1⅔fl oz (50ml) juice	Alfalfa sprouts
Excellent source of dietary fiber and nature's perfect cleanser. High in vitamin C and contains vitamins A (mostly in the skin) and B.	1 apple = 3½fl oz (100ml) juice	Apple
One of the best natural sources of vitamins A and C; full of potassium.	1 apricot = 1 Tbsp (15ml) juice	Apricot
Arugula supplies folate and some calcium. It also contains beta-carotene and vitamin C.	1 bunch arugula = 2 Tbsp juice	Arugula (rocket)
One of the most energy-dense and nutrient-rich fruits per calorie. Excellent source of folic acid; good source of vitamin B6.	1 avocado = 4fl oz (125ml) blended pulp	Avocado

Ingredient	Seasonality	Storage tips/juicing preparation
Banana	A winter fruit produced mainly in India, Brazil, the Philippines and Indonesia. Temperature-controlled transport compartments make year-round export possible.	Bananas are delicate and don't like sudden temperature changes. Store at room temperature. Refrigeration will brown their skin, but not the banana within.
Beetroot	Season stretches through the summer. Clipped tops means beets have been in storage and are less tender. Also sold boiled, often dipped in vinegar and vacuum sealed.	Fresh beetroot will keep 2–4 weeks if cool or refrigerated. Clip leafy tops and store 3–5 days in refrigerator.
Blackberry	Blackberries are a summer fruit grown in North America, Europe and Australia, but are available off-season, at an expense.	Blackberries are highly perishable. Spoiled berries will ruin surrounding fruit. Store in the refrigerator, unwashed and loosely packed. Best when freshly picked from the bush.
Blackcurrant	A summer berry. Major producers are Germany, Poland and Russia.	Will keep in the refrigerator for up to 3 days. Blackcurrants freeze well and are often sold frozen. Thaw slightly before juicing.

Benefits	Approximate juice yield	Ingredient
Bananas are rich in fiber, potassium and vitamins C and B6.	1 banana = 4fl oz (125ml) juice	Banana
Beetroot contains folate, potassium and manganese. The green leafy tops are especially nutritious, as they contain calcium, beta-carotene and iron.	1 beetroot with leaves = 1⅔fl oz (50ml) juice	Beetroot
Blackberries are an excellent source of vitamin E, which is beneficial for heart and circulatory problems.	1 handful = 2½fl oz (75ml) juice	Blackberry
Contains four times as much vitamin C as oranges. A rich source of potassium, beneficial in the treatment of high blood pressure. Skin contains anthocyanoside, an antibacterial pigment which is good for sore throats.	1 handful = 1⅔fl oz (50ml) juice	Blackcurrant

Ingredient	Seasonality	Storage tips/juicing preparation
Blueberry	Late summer fruit. Wild blueberries are available fresh in late summer throughout eastern Canada and the eastern United States. Cultivated blueberries are grown throughout parts of Europe.	Both wild and cultivated varieties are the least perishable of berries and will keep for up to 10 days in the refrigerator. Blueberries freeze well and are often sold frozen. Thaw slightly before juicing.
Cabbage (baby)	A sturdy, winter, leafy green related to kale, broccoli, collards and brussels sprouts, to name only a few.	Cabbages will keep for up to 2 weeks, wrapped and stored separately, in the refrigerator.
Carrot	Carrots, a classic root vegetable, are now available year-round. The largest producers are China, USA, Poland, Japan, France and England.	Carrots will keep for 1–3 weeks in the refrigerator. Store in a brown paper or perforated plastic bag.
Celery	Celery is traditionally harvested in the summer months, but is now available year-round. The English love the white-fleshed varieties, while darker green celery is favored by the North American palate.	Store celery for up to a week in the refrigerator, preferably wrapped in a plastic bag.
Celeriac	Also known as celery root, celeriac is harvested in autumn-winter, but is available, along with other root vegetables, almost year-round. Cultivated mainly in Europe, but also in Asia and parts of North America.	Store celeriac in the refrigerator or in a cool, dry place for up to 2 weeks. Wash well before juicing – soil tends to hide in the tufts and rootlets.

Benefits	Approximate juice yield	Ingredient
Blueberries contain more disease-fighting, age-proofing antioxidants than practically any other fruit or vegetable. Antioxidant strength is found in the blue skin.	1 handful = 1fl oz (30ml) juice	Blueberry
A good source of beta-carotene, folic acid, vitamin C, iron, potassium and sodium; also a powerful antioxidant and cleanser.	1 head = 5fl oz (150ml) juice	Cabbage (baby)
Known as the richest source of beta-carotene, carrots are also a good source of vitamin C, calcium and potassium. They cleanse the liver, increase energy and aid eye and skin problems.	1 medium carrot = 1⅔fl oz (50ml) juice	Carrot
Crispy celery ribs contain massive amounts of water and smaller amounts of potassium, folic acid and vitamin C. Celery cleanses, calms and rebuilds red blood cells.	1 stalk = 3½fl oz (100ml) juice	Celery
Celeriac is a good source of vitamins B6 and C, potassium, iron and magnesium.	1 celeriac = 7fl oz (200 ml) juice	Celeriac

Ingredient	Seasonality	Storage tips/juicing preparation
Cherry	Cherries are best eaten in summer, when they're at their seasonal peak. The Bing cherry is most common in North America; the Bigaroon and Gean cherries, both sweet varieties, are most popular in Europe.	Cherries spoil quickly, but will keep in the refrigerator for 2–3 days. Cherries can be bought or stored frozen.
Chicory (endive)	Harvested in the autumn in parts of North America, France, Holland, Belgium and Italy.	Soaking chicory removes the bitterness – simply wipe clean with a cloth. Store loosely in the refrigerator for 3–5 days.
Chili pepper	Chili peppers are cultivated on all continents, grown as a perennial in tropical regions and as an annual in temperate zones. Major producers are Mexico and the West Indies.	Peppers are happiest wrapped in a paper bag and stored in the refrigerator for up to 7 days.
Coriander (cilantro)	Fresh coriander is available year-round, or locally throughout the summer months. Look for greens with roots attached.	Wrap fresh coriander with roots in a damp paper towel, place inside a plastic bag and store in the refrigerator for 2–3 days.
Cranberry	Most of the commercial cranberry crop (harvested in the USA and Canada) is juiced, canned or frozen. Look for fresh cranberries in the autumn.	Cranberries store well. Store in the refrigerator for up to 2 weeks or in the freezer for up to 1 year.

Benefits	Approximate juice yield	Ingredient
Rich in folic acid, beta-carotene, vitamin C and calcium; also packed with pectin, a soluble fiber that helps control blood cholesterol levels.	1 handful = 2½fl oz (75ml)	Cherry
Chicory (endive) is an excellent source of folic acid and potassium. It stimulates the appetite and cleanses the digestive system.	1 head = 2½fl oz (75ml) juice	Chicory (endive)
Chilies have a significant amount of vitamin C; capsaicin (compound that makes chilies hot) has a positive effect on blood cholesterol and also works as an anticoagulant.	1 chili = ½ tsp juice	Chili pepper
Soothes digestion, acts as a diuretic, reduces cholesterol and improves eyesight.	1 bunch = 2 Tbsp juice	Coriander (cilantro)
Rich in beta-carotene, folic acid, vitamin C, calcium, chlorine, magnesium, phosphorus and potassium. Soothes the digestive and urinary tract.	1 handful = 1⅔fl oz (50ml) juice	Cranberry

Ingredient	Seasonality	Storage tips/juicing preparation
Cucumber	Cucumbers are at their best from late spring through mid-summer, but are available, thanks to greenhouses, year-round.	Wrap cucumbers tightly in plastic and store in the refrigerator for up to 1 week. Discard wilted ends before juicing and remove any waxy skin.
Feijoa	Feijoa is a fruit native to South America, but today New Zealand is the world's largest producer. Look for them in spring and early winter.	Store feijoa at room temperature until ripe. Consume immediately when ripe, or store in the refrigerator for 2–3 days. Peel before juicing.
Fennel	Look for fennel in the autumn and winter months. Most fennel is exported from Italy.	Fennel can be kept in the refrigerator for up to 1 week, but will become stringy and lose its flavor over time. Choose firm, fragrant, white bulbs with fresh, green stems.
Fig	Figs – purple, black and green varieties – are produced in Turkey, Greece, USA, Portugal and Spain. They are harvested in late summer.	Fresh figs are highly perishable. Store in the refrigerator for 2–3 days, and consume when ripe.
Grape	There are many varieties of grapes, each with their own season. Most table grapes are harvested in southern Europe and the USA in the autumn.	Grapes wilt at room temperature. Store in a perforated plastic bag in the refrigerator for up to 3 days. If using a blender, use seedless grapes, but any kind of grape can be used in a juicer.
Grapefruit	Most of the world's grapefruit crop is harvested in winter and exported from Florida.	Grapefruit will keep refrigerated for 6–8 weeks or at room temperature for 1 week. They're juiciest at room temperature.

Benefits	Approximate juice yield	Ingredient
Rich in folic acid, calcium, chlorine and small amounts of vitamins B1, 2, 3, 5 and 6. Highly diuretic, cleansing and beneficial for hair, skin and nails.	1 medium cucumber = 18fl oz (500ml) juice	Cucumber
Feijoa is a good source of folic acid, vitamin C and potassium.	1 feijoa = 2½fl oz (75ml) juice	Feijoa
Rich in vitamin C, potassium, calcium and, in lesser amounts, vitamin B6. Cleanses digestive tract, soothes gastric pain, is a diuretic and a stimulant.	1 fennel bulb = 3½fl oz (100ml) juice	Fennel
Rich in folic acid, beta-carotene, calcium, iron and potassium. Juice is a digestive tract cleanser.	1 fig = 1fl oz (30ml) juice	Fig
Grapes are rich in vitamins C and E, calcium, antioxidants, phosphorus, flavonoids and potassium. They cleanse the digestive system and clear the skin.	1 bunch grapes = 2½fl oz (75ml) juice	Grape
A cleansing juice rich in beta-carotene, calcium, potassium and vitamin C.	1 grapefruit = 3½fl oz (100ml) juice	Grapefruit

Ingredient	Seasonality	Storage tips/juicing preparation
Guava	Guavas predominate in tropical and sub-tropical regions such as Hawaii and India. They are available all-year-round in warmer climates with an abundance during late spring and summer.	For the best flavor the fruit should ripen on the tree. They can be picked green-mature and allowed to ripen off the tree at room temperature. Once ripe, the fruit will bruise easily and quickly deteriorate. When ripe, use within 3–4 days.
Iceberg lettuce	One of the most common lettuces, iceberg is available year-round.	Iceberg is a sturdy lettuce that will keep well, refrigerated, for up to 10 days.
Kiwi fruit	Ten varieties are cultivated each year; mainly in New Zealand, USA, Europe, South America and Australia.	Leave kiwi fruits to ripen at room temperature until they are slightly soft. Unripe kiwis will keep, refrigerated, for 2–3 weeks.
Leek	Leeks, the national vegetable of Wales, are best in later summer, but are available year-round.	Leeks will keep, refrigerated, for up to 2 weeks. They will keep in cold, dry storage for up to 3 months.
Lemon	The bulk of the world's lemons are acidic and are harvested year-round in California.	Lemons will keep at room temperature for 1 week, or for up to 10 days if refrigerated. Peel before juicing.
Lime	Lime trees flower and bear fruit all year. Major producers are Mexico, West Indies, USA, India, Spain and Italy.	Limes will last for up to 5 days at room temperature, or up to 9 days if refrigerated. Peel before juicing.

Benefits	Approximate juice yield	Ingredient
Guavas are extremely high in vitamin C. Amounts can be five times as high as that of fresh oranges. Also rich in beta-carotene.	1 guava = 1fl oz (30ml) juice	Guava
A good source of folic acid, vitamin C and potassium. Its juice is detoxifying and calming.	1 head = 7fl oz (200ml) juice	Iceberg lettuce
Rich in beta-carotene and vitamin C. Kiwi juice is also an excellent cleanser and energizer.	1 kiwi fruit = 1½fl oz (40ml) juice	Kiwi fruit
Rich in beta-carotene, vitamin C, folic acid, calcium and biotin.	1 leek = 1fl oz (30ml) juice	Leek
An excellent source of vitamin C, beta-carotene, calcium, magnesium and very cleansing for the liver and kidneys.	1 lemon = 1fl oz (30ml) juice	Lemon
Rich in beta-carotene, folic acid, vitamin C and calcium.	1 lime = 1fl oz (30ml) juice	Lime

Ingredient	Seasonality	Storage tips/juicing preparation
Lychee (litchi)	A native, "good luck" fruit from China, they are now produced in Southeast Asia, South Africa, Australia, Israel, Mexico and USA.	Lychees will keep for several weeks in a plastic bag in the refrigerator, but are best when ripe – pinkish-red in color. Split shell and peel before juicing.
Mange-tout (snow pea)	Fresh mange-touts are best in late spring, but are available in large or Asian markets year-round.	Store in a plastic bag in the refrigerator for 3–5 days.
Mango	Mangoes are a summer fruit, imported mainly from Thailand, India, Pakistan and Mexico.	Mangoes keep well. Ripen at room temperature. Once ripened (soft), consume or refrigerate for up to 1 week.
Melon	Melons, a summer fruit, grow in temperate regions. Off-season they are often harvested before ripening for transport, but they will not ripen properly once picked, so choose carefully.	Look for melons with smooth skin, free of cracks and bruises. The stalk ends should be soft and their smell should be gentle but fragrant. Melons will soften at room temperature. Once cut, refrigerate.
Nectarine	The bulk of nectarines are produced in the USA and are at their prime in mid-summer.	Ripen nectarines at room temperature. Once soft and ripe, refrigerate for 1–3 days.
Orange	Best during the winter months, when Floridian, Spanish and Israeli oranges are at their best.	Store in a cool, dry place. Unless using a peel-friendly industrial juicer, peel all citrus fruits before juicing.

Benefits	Approximate juice yield	Ingredient
Lychees are rich in vitamin C and are a good source of potassium.	1 lychee = 1fl oz (30ml) juice	Lychee (litchi)
Good source of iron, vitamin C, folic acid, magnesium and thiamine.	1 mange-tout = 1 tsp juice	Mange-tout (snow pea)
Rich in vitamins B and C, beta-carotene, calcium, magnesium and phosphorus.	1 mango = 3½fl oz (100ml) juice	Mango
Rich in beta-carotene, folic acid, calcium, magnesium; melon juice is cleansing and diuretic.	1 melon = 14fl oz (400ml) juice	Melon
An energizing, antioxidant juice, rich in beta-carotene, vitamin C, folic acid, calcium and magnesium.	1 nectarine = 2½fl oz (75ml) juice	Nectarine
High in antioxidants and vitamin C.	1 orange = 3½fl oz (100ml) juice	Orange

Ingredient	Seasonality	Storage tips/juicing preparation
Papaya (paw paw)	Papayas are a spring fruit, produced in tropical and subtropical climes, such as Brazil, Mexico, Thailand, Indonesia and India.	Leave to ripen at room temperature and consume when ripe, or store for up to 3 days in the refrigerator.
Passion fruit	Passion fruit grow in tropical regions: New Zealand, Africa, Malaysia and West Indies.	The hard shell will wrinkle when ripe. Store at room temperature to ripen. Cut open and scoop out flesh for juicing.
Peach	Peaches are a summer fruit and grow in warm climates; mainly USA, Italy, China and Greece.	Peaches will spoil quickly once bruised, so handle with care. Store loosely; allow to ripen at room temperature. Once ripe, consume within 2–3 days.
Pear	Best in the autumn and winter months.	Store pears at room temperature, but watch carefully, as they ripen and spoil quickly. Best juiced when crunchy, firm and slightly unripe.
Pepper (sweet, bell, capsicum)	Today, peppers are available year-round, exported mainly from China, Turkey, Spain and Mexico.	Peppers will keep for a week in the refrigerator. Store whole to maintain their flavor and nutrients. Remove stalk, core and seeds before juicing.
Persimmon (sharon, kaki)	Persimmons are a late autumn-winter fruit, which hail from the USA, Asia and Israel.	Persimmons will ripen at room temperature. Once ripened, (soft and red) store at room temperature. They can be frozen whole, or juiced/blended, then frozen.

Benefits	Approximate juice yield	Ingredient
Rich in beta-carotene, vitamin C, calcium and magnesium. Juice is an antioxidant. Energizes and cleanses the digestive tract.	1 papaya = 7fl oz (200ml) juice	Papaya (paw paw)
Rich in calcium, beta-carotene, vitamin B3 and magnesium.	1 passion fruit = 1 Tbsp juice	Passion fruit
An excellent source of folic acid, beta-carotene, vitamins B3 and C, niacin, calcium and flavonoids.	1 peach = 2½fl oz (75ml) juice	Peach
Rich in fiber, contain potassium.	1 pear = 2½fl oz (75ml) juice (when an over-ripe pear is juiced, the yield is thick and small)	Pear
Rich in beta-carotene, folic acid, vitamin C and calcium. They cleanse the system and benefit hair, skin and nails.	1 pepper = 1⅔fl oz (50ml) juice	Pepper (sweet, bell, capsicum)
Good source of vitamin A; contain potassium, vitamin C, copper and have a mild laxative effect.	1 persimmon = 3½fl oz (100ml) juice	Persimmon (sharon, kaki)

Ingredient	Seasonality	Storage tips/juicing preparation
Pineapple	Pineapples are produced in most tropical regions, namely Central and South America, Australia, the Pacific Islands, Asia and Africa, and shipped around the world. Winter is their natural season.	Pineapples, despite their gruff exterior, are delicate and bruise easily. The fruit ferments quickly at room temperature. They will keep in the refrigerator, in a plastic bag, for 3–5 days.
Plum	Plums are available locally in temperate climates in the spring; off-season, various varieties are imported from the USA, Russia, China and Eastern Europe.	Plums can be left at room temperature to ripen; when ripe, store in the refrigerator for up to 3 days.
Pomegranate	Best during the autumn months. Pick fruit up and feel its weight – the seeds represent 52% of the whole fruit weight. Choose heavy pomegranates with shiny, taut and thin skins without cracks or splits.	Store in a cool, dark place for up to a month and in the refrigerator for up to 2 months. Seeds can be refrigerated for up to 3 days or frozen in an airtight container for up to 6 months.
Quince	Quinces – a cross between a pear and an apple – grow in warm climates and are harvested in the autumn.	Quinces turn from green to yellow as they ripen. Leave to ripen at room temperature.
Radicchio	Radicchio is an autumn plant, grown primarily in the south of France and Italy.	Radicchio will keep in the refrigerator, in a plastic bag, for up to 1 week.

Benefits	Approximate juice yield	Ingredient
Pineapple juice cleanses the intestines, boosts the immune system and is rich in beta-carotene, folic acid and vitamin C.	1 pineapple = 15fl oz (450ml) juice	Pineapple
The antioxidants in plum juice boost the immune system, which stimulates the appetite. Plums are also rich in beta-carotene, vitamins C and E and folic acid.	1 plum = 1fl oz (30ml) juice	Plum
Seeds are a good source of potassium and vitamin C. Its tart flavor comes from the high content of citric acid.	1 pomegranate = 4fl oz (125ml) juice (5oz/150g seeds)	Pomegranate
A good source of potassium, vitamin C and copper.	1 quince = 4fl oz (125ml) juice	Quince
Radicchio contains folic acid, copper, potassium and vitamin C. It cleanses the blood and stimulates the appetite.	1 head radicchio = 2½fl oz (75ml) juice	Radicchio

Ingredient	Seasonality	Storage tips/juicing preparation
Radish	Red and white radishes are sold year-round, but supplies are most plentiful during the spring months. Choose well-shaped radishes with crisp, green leaves and with good color.	Unless consuming on the day of purchase you should remove the leaves. Radishes will keep for up to 2 weeks in the refrigerator in a plastic bag. Scrub well, but leave skins on for juicing.
Raspberry	Raspberries are readily available in summer, but imports can generally be bought year-round at an expense. Choose berries very carefully – observe the container for dampness or stains indicating the fruit may be crushed or decaying. They should be plump, firm, well-shaped and uniformly colored.	Raspberries should be used within 1–2 days of purchasing. Raspberries also freeze very well. Spread them in a single layer and freeze until solid before transferring to a bag – they will keep for 10–12 months.
Spinach	Fresh spinach is available all year-round but grows best during the winter months. Select small spinach leaves with a good green color and crisp, springy texture. Look for thin, not coarse, stems.	Fresh spinach will keep for 3–4 days in the refrigerator. Make sure you wash thoroughly before juicing and remove any tough stalks.

Benefits	Approximate juice yield	Ingredient
Radishes are a good source of vitamin C.	1 radish = 1fl oz (30ml)	Radish
Raspberries are packed with fiber – some in its soluble form, pectin. Also high in phytochemicals and a good source of vitamin C.	1 handful = 2½fl oz (75ml) juice	Raspberry
Spinach is exceptionally rich in carotenoids. Also rich in folate, potassium, magnesium and manganese. Spinach contains more protein than most vegetables.	1 bunch = 1fl oz (30ml) juice	Spinach

Ingredient	Seasonality	Storage tips/juicing preparation
Spring onion (green onion, scallion)	Spring onions are harvested before the onion bulb has a chance to mature. They are available year-round, but are best in mid-summer.	Spring onions, unlike mature onions, are quite perishable. Store in a plastic bag in the refrigerator for up to 3 days and consume before green tops have a chance to wilt.
Squash (butternut)	Winter squash (thick skins) are harvested in the autumn, but are fresh through the winter months.	Winter squash will keep for several months if stored in a cool, dark place.
Strawberry	Most delicious when purchased locally in the summer months, but are available shipped from warmer climes throughout the year.	Strawberries are very perishable. Store in the refrigerator – making sure there aren't any spoiled berries in the pack – for 2–3 days.
Sweet potato	Sweet potatoes are available throughout the year but are most abundant in autumn and early winter. Select sweet potatoes that are heavy for their size, smooth, hard and free of bruises and decay.	Sweet potatoes should be stored in a cool, dry place – never refrigerated. They will keep for 1 month. If kept at normal room temperature, they should be used within a week of purchase. Wash off excess dirt before juicing.

Benefits	Approximate juice yield	Ingredient
Onions are known as a panacea for their myriad medicinal qualities. Spring onions contain potassium, folic acid and vitamin C, to name a few.	1 spring onion = 1 tsp juice	Spring onion (green onion, scallion)
Squashes are an excellent source of potassium and vitamin A, and a good source of vitamin C and folic acid.	1 squash = 3½fl oz (100ml) juice	Squash (butternut)
Strawberries are rich in beta-carotene, folic acid, vitamins C and E, and are cleansing and energizing.	1 handful = 2½fl oz (75ml) juice	Strawberry
Sweet potatoes are rich in beta-carotene. Excellent source of fiber with skin on – about half of which is soluble. Also good source of vitamins C and B6, manganese and potassium.	1 sweet potato = 3½fl oz (100ml) juice	Sweet potato

Ingredient	Seasonality	Storage tips/juicing preparation
Tamarillo (tree tomato)	Available in autumn and winter, but grown in California and New Zealand and can be obtained year-round. Look for well-colored fruit that gives just slightly to finger pressure.	Ripen at room temperature if too firm. Tamarillo should be peeled before juicing. Immerse in boiling water for 3–5 minutes to loosen the skin.
Tomato	There are thousands of tomato varieties available which are bred in a variety of climates. Available all year-round. Choose red tomatoes – look for plump, heavy tomatoes with smooth skins. Never buy tomatoes from a refrigerated case.	Tomatoes should be stored at room temperature. Do not refrigerate. To ripen tomatoes, place in a brown paper bag with an apple or a banana; they give off ethylene gas.
Watercress	Watercress is available in well-stocked supermarkets throughout the year, but as it grows in fresh-water streams, it is in season in the summer months.	Watercress is perishable and should be consumed as soon as possible. Wrap in a damp paper towel and store in the refrigerator for no more than 2 days.
Watermelon	Watermelons grow in warm climates and are in season throughout the summer months.	Watermelons will become dry and fibrous inside if left to ripen in the heat. Store in the refrigerator or a cool, dry place and consume as soon as possible.

Benefits	Approximate juice yield	Ingredient
Tamarillos are a good source of fiber, beta-carotene and vitamin C.	1 tamarillo = 2fl oz (60ml) juice	Tamarillo (tree tomato)
Tomatoes are a delicious source of vitamin C. They are one of the best sources of lycopene – a carotenoid with cancer-fighting properties.	1 tomato = 1⅔fl oz (50ml) juice	Tomato
Watercress is full of vitamins A and C and potassium. Its juice is diuretic, cleanses the intestines and stimulates the appetite.	1 handful watercress = 1fl oz (30ml) juice	Watercress
Rich in beta-carotene, folic acid, calcium, magnesium, phosphorus and potassium. It is also a cleansing diuretic.	1.2kg watermelon = 1¼pt (800ml) juice	Watermelon

Herbal remedies

We are undergoing a health revolution. As more people take responsibility for their own health, the demand for natural foods, herbal medicines and nutraceuticals is growing dramatically. We have focused on only a fraction of what is available on today's market. By no means do we claim, nor have the authority to claim, that any of these herbal remedies are a suitable alternative to medicated drugs. We believe that the use of herbal remedies, in moderation, may enhance well-being and, in many cases, may help counter other ailments and illnesses. It is fundamental that dosages are taken as recommended by the manufacturers, as potency and composition of products vary considerably. You should also check that the product is suitable for you as some products are not suitable for children, pregnant or breast-feeding women, those with an existing medical condition or who are on medication.

Wheatgrass

Wheatgrass is the latest craze in juices and health drinks. Every reputable juice bar in town seems to have these green blades prominently placed and growing on their counters. Wheatgrass, the grains of wheat that have sprouted until they become young grass, usually grows to 3–4in (7.5–10cm) high. It is said to be cleansing, detoxifying and immune-boosting – an all-round natural tonic.

Wheatgrass, when juiced or puréed, forms an intensely green juice containing many nutrients, antioxidants and high amounts of chlorophyll. The molecular composition of chlorophyll is so close to that of human hemoglobin that these drinks can act as "mini transfusions" for the blood and tonics for the brain and immune system. We believe that green, high chlorophyll drinks are critical to the success of every cleansing program. If it is not available fresh, wheatgrass can be bought freeze-dried and used according to the manufacturers' recommendations.

Spirulina

Spirulina is a microscopic algae in the shape of a perfect coil. Although this ancient algae has been known and eaten for centuries, it was rediscovered by scientists 30 years ago and is now being called a "superfood." Spirulina contains the highest concentration of nutrients known in any one food, plant, grain or herb. It contains over 60 percent of all digestible vegetable proteins making it the highest protein food available to us. It also has the highest concentration of beta-carotene, vitamin B12, iron, trace minerals and the rare essential fatty acid, GLA. The amount of each nutrient that you actually obtain from one measure of spirulina is, however, minimal, making it an expensive superfood. Spirulina is available from health food stores in powder and capsule form and should only be taken according to the manufacturers' recommendations.

Honey

Honey, pollen, propolis and beeswax have been used by humankind for both nutritional and medicinal consumption for thousands of years. Bees gather the sugary nectar of flowers, modify it and store it in honeycomb. The flavor and aroma of honey depends entirely on the flowers from which the nectar has been obtained. Honey is beneficial in juicing as a natural, unrefined sweetener and also for its medicinal and antiseptic properties in its unheated state. One of our preferred honey types is Manuka honey, obtained from the flowers of the Manuka bush, which is indigenous to New Zealand. The honey-making process is enriched by the pollution-free environment of New Zealand.

Manuka honey is renowned for its special antibacterial properties. The honey has proved effective in the treatment of a range of problems in which bacteria or fungal infection play a role. It is now being used to combat the antibiotic-resistant bacteria MRSA which infects surgical wounds in hospital wards.

Royal jelly

Honey is one of the oldest foods known to humans, but more recently the popularity of royal jelly has led to new and astonishing discoveries. Royal jelly is the sole food fed to the chosen Queen bee by worker bees. It has been revealed that the astonishing longevity (3–5 years as opposed to 6–8 weeks), fertility (laying around 20 eggs per day) and endurance of the Queen bee is entirely due to her exclusive diet of nutrient-rich royal jelly. There is no real evidence that royal jelly has the same effect on humans but it certainly seems worth a try.

Royal jelly contains proteins, amino acids and B vitamins, in addition to vitamins A, C, D and E and traces of natural minerals. It may help to develop a great feeling of well-being, boost energy levels and strengthen the immune system. Anyone who is considering supplementing their juices with royal jelly should consult a qualified medical practitioner, especially those who are allergic to bee stings, honey or those with asthma. Royal jelly is available from health-food specialists in capsule and extract form and should be taken according to the manufacturers' recommendations.

Ginkgo biloba
It is the leaves of the gingko biloba tree that are thought to be beneficial to maintain brain function. Ginkgo biloba oxygenates the blood increasing mental alertness, memory and concentration. Blood flow is also increased to the hands and feet. This is particularly useful for the elderly but should be avoided if pregnant. Ginkgo biloba can be bought in extract, dried leaf or tablet form and should be taken according to the manufacturers' recommendations.

Ginger
Ginger has been cultivated in China and India for thousands of years and has been recommended by Chinese herbalists for more than 2,500 years. It is the root of the ginger plant – either in fresh, dried or extract form – that proves to be beneficial for a number of ailments. Commonly used to aid digestion, alleviate motion sickness and reduce nausea, ginger is a well recognized remedy. During pregnancy ginger acts as an antispasmodic and helps prevent nausea and vomiting associated with

morning sickness. It is also useful for post-anesthesia associated nausea. It also acts as an anti-inflammatory and is used in the treatment of arthritis and other inflammatory joint diseases. As with garlic we believe that "fresh is best," but if unavailable, capsule, dried and extract form can be taken according to the manufacturers' recommendations.

Garlic
Garlic has been used as a food and as an herb since 3,000 BC by the Egyptians, Romans and Vikings. It was also used extensively during times of war, particularly the First World War, for its therapeutic properties when antibiotics were in short supply. Garlic is so prevalent in our diet that we often overlook its nutritional benefits.

Garlic is one of the most popular and widely used herbs in the world today. It contains phytochemicals, including allicin, which may help combat heart disease by helping lower serum cholesterol levels. Experts say that the active ingredients in garlic are extremely volatile and are destroyed during cooking. We highly recommend the use of fresh garlic in our juices, but it is available in capsule and extract form at greater costs. Fresh is best.

Lavender
Lavender is a shrubby indigenous plant most commonly found in

the mountainous regions of western Mediterranean countries. Originally cultivated in parts of France and Italy for its aromatic flowers, lavender has been used in perfumes and as a condiment and flavoring for dishes because of its "comfort to the stomach." It has aromatic, carminative and nervine properties. We have used fresh lavender in our recipes, but it is available for consumption in tablet form and should be taken according to the manufacturers' recommendations.

Ginseng

Ginseng is the most popular food supplement from the East. The root of the ginseng plant was highly prized by early Chinese emperors as having many uses, primarily as a tonic or stimulant for both mental and physical disorders and for its stress-relieving qualities. There are two main types of ginseng available on the market – *panax* ginseng, also called Korean ginseng, and Siberian ginseng. It is thought that both types of ginseng can help the body fight or adapt to whatever problems it has. Also known as the "magical root," this stimulant is often used to help reduce stress levels. Recent studies also claim that ginseng may help regulate blood glucose levels and be beneficial for diabetes sufferers. Ginseng is available in extract, capsule and tea form, and dosages should be taken according

to the manufacturers' recommendations.

Echinacea

Echinacea is a relatively recent medicinal herb to have made it into the global spotlight. In the Western world it is now the most popular immune-boosting herb available. Echinacea stimulates the immune system by increasing the white blood cells' ability to overpower invading organisms. This herb also stimulates the lymphatic system to regenerate tissue and decrease inflammation, particularly that caused by rheumatoid arthritis.

Echinacea comes in capsule, extract and tea forms, and dosage should only be taken according to the manufacturers' recommendations.

Gotu kola

Gotu kola was probably first used in India, as part of Ayurveda, the traditional herbal medicine, but is now widely available in the Western world. Gotu kola is known as the "memory herb." It stimulates circulation to the brain and was traditionally used to promote longevity, as a blood cleanser and a diuretic. Gotu kola is considered to be one of the best nerve tonics, and many people use it to increase learning ability. It promotes mental calm and assists in the practice of yoga or meditation. Gotu kola is available in capsule and extract form and should only be taken according to the manufacturers' recommendations.

Flaxseed oil (linseed oil)

A source of fiber for linen fabrics since ancient times, the flax plant also boasts a long history as a healing herb. Flaxseeds, also called linseeds, are best known for their oil that has been derived by pressing them. Flaxseed is a useful herbal remedy for vegetarians and non-fish eaters. It is the richest source of the omega-3 essential fatty acid, alpha linolenic acid, and can be converted in the body to the fatty acids EPA and DHA, which are those present in fish. It appears to reduce the risk of heart disease and numerous other ailments. Flaxseeds are available in ground form and as oil and should only be taken according to the manufacturers' recommendations.

Milk thistles

The milk thistle plant is native to the Mediterranean and grows wild throughout Europe, North America and Australia. Milk thistle has been used in Europe as a remedy for liver problems for thousands of years.

As our lives have become more exposed to the detrimental effects of environmental toxins, alcohol, drugs and chemotherapy, we have turned back to this age-old herb for assistance. Milk thistle has been proven to protect the liver from damage and may counter these environmental factors. It is the active component, silybin, which functions as an antioxidant and is one of the most potent liver protective agents known to humans. Not only does it inhibit the factors responsible for liver damage, but it stimulates the production of new liver cells to replace old damaged ones. Milk thistle is available from health-food specialists in extract and powder form and should only be taken according to the manufacturers' recommendations.

Live yogurt (pro-biotics)

Our intestinal tract is home to billions of bacteria comprising hundreds of beneficial species. These friendly micro-organisms are called pro-biotics, meaning "for life" and *acidophilus*, *lactobacillus* and *lactobacillus bifidus* fall into this category. Above all, pro-biotics help us to get more nutrition out of the food we eat. Live yogurts contain pro-biotics and consequently help promote intestinal health. It is important to buy live yogurt from a refrigerated supplier, as the friendly bacteria can easily be destroyed if exposed to heat and light. These bacteria are also available in tablet form and should be taken according to the manufacturers' recommendations.

Herbs – *sage, mint, coriander, rosemary, parsley*

In the Western world we tend to think of herbs only as flavorings, very much like we do salt and pepper. We are the culprits of having jars of dried herbs in our pantries for a long time past their use-by date and often take for granted the flavor and health benefits of fresh herbs. Fresh herbs have many medicinal properties that can be a beneficial addition to our daily diets.

Spices – *cayenne, juniper berries, chili, cinnamon, cloves, nutmeg, black pepper, saffron, vanilla*

Spices are extremely difficult to define. Spices, in contrast to herbs, are almost always, although not invariably, used in dried form. Spices are usually the rhizome, root, bark, flower, fruit or seeds of the plant. Herbs in comparison are usually the herbaceous or leafy parts of the same plant.

Spices have been of great interest and importance in history – during the spice trade they were very important in commercial terms and sometimes used as currency. In commercial terms, pepper, cloves and nutmeg have always ruled the hierarchy. In culinary and medicinal terms spices are also very important. Spices take up relatively little space in your pantry, and their distinct flavors can often make or break your dish. Medicinally they individually provide benefits to counter many ailments and can easily be added to juices and smoothies.

Nuts and seeds – *almonds, pine nuts, sesame seeds, poppy seeds*

Nuts and seeds are both highly nutritious food sources. Small amounts can provide plenty of energy. All nuts contribute significant amounts of iron, zinc and magnesium. Protein is also found in good amounts, particularly in peanuts and almonds. Most nuts have a high monounsaturated fat content which is beneficial in maintaining blood cholesterol levels. Hazelnuts and macadamias contain the highest sources of monounsaturated fats. Seeds mainly contain polyunsaturated fats, but due to their light weight only a small sprinkling is usually required.

Nutritional benefits

Vitamins and minerals are nutrients that your body needs to work properly. They boost the immune system, are essential for normal growth and development and help cells and organs do their jobs. Vitamins and minerals are found in the foods we eat, and fruits and vegetables are no exception. In the following pages we have outlined the benefits and sources of many of the vitamins and minerals that are essential to maintain a healthy body and mind.

Vitamins

	Benefits	Source
Vitamin A	Vitamin A helps maintain healthy eyes, skin and bones. It promotes a healthy immune system and is essential for the growth and development of cells. *Deficiency may result in poor teeth and bone growth, night blindness and diarrhea.*	Dark green leafy vegetables such as spinach and broccoli. Deep orange fruits such as carrots, sweet potatoes, oranges, pumpkin, apricots, papayas and mangoes.
Vitamin C	Vitamin C is an important antioxidant that helps mop up free radicals in the body. It helps with wound-healing by forming connective tissues and promoting healthy capillaries. Vitamin C also aids in strengthening resistance against infection and certain illnesses. Vitamin C aids the body's absorption of iron and calcium. *Deficiency may result in anemia, infections, sore gums, muscle and joint pain.*	Citrus fruits, dark green leafy vegetables, strawberries, kiwi, peppers, tomatoes, potatoes and guavas.

	Benefits	Source
Vitamin B6	Vitamin B6 helps form red blood cells and is important in maintaining a healthy nervous system and a functioning brain. It also helps the body build amino acids and proteins that are needed for proper growth and development. *Deficiency may result in skin disorders, muscle-twitching, anemia or cracks at corners of mouth.*	Green leafy vegetables, eggs, bananas and avocados.
Vitamin B2 (Riboflavin)	Riboflavin is essential in the body for production of energy. It also aids normal growth of body tissues, promoting healthy skin and supporting vision. *Deficiency may result in sensitive eyes, skin rash or cracks at the corners of the mouth.*	Dark green leafy vegetables, broccoli, asparagus, avocados, almonds, whole grains, dried fruit and dairy products.
Folate	Folate is essential for normal tissue growth and for keeping cells healthy. *Deficiency may result in anemia, constipation, diarrhea, infections, confusion, weakness, smooth red tongue.*	Leafy green vegetables, nuts, fortified orange juice.
Vitamin E	Vitamin E is an important anitoxidant and helps stabilize cell membranes. *Deficiency may result in anemia and weakness.*	Green leafy vegetables, egg yolk and whole grain products.

Minerals

	Benefits	Source
Calcium	Calcium is vital for building strong bones and teeth. *Deficiency may result in stunted growth in children and weakened bone density in adults.*	Dairy products, such as milk and yogurt.
Iron	Iron helps produce hemoglobin which carries oxygen around the body. *Deficiency may result in recurring headaches, chronic fatigue, irritability, anemia and infections.*	Green leafy vegetables, dried fruits and egg yolk.
Magnesium	Magnesium is important in the development of bones and teeth, transmits nerve impulses important in muscle contraction and activates enzymes needed for energy. *Deficiency may result in weakness, confusion and growth failure in children.*	Dark green leafy vegetables, whole grains and nuts.
Manganese	Manganese is important for healthy cell functioning. It works with enzymes to help with many cell processes. *Even trace amounts of manganese do not produce deficiencies in the body.*	Most fruits and vegetables, whole grains and nuts.

	Benefits	Source
Potassium	Potassium is important in maintaining fluid balance, transmission of nerve impulses and helps in the making of protein. *Deficiency may result in muscle weakness, fatigue and confusion.*	Most fruits and vegetables, particularly bananas, and milk.

Bibliography

Braimbridge, Sophie and Copeland, Jennie, *Energy Food*, Murdoch Books UK, 2002.

Davidson, Alan, *The Penguin Companion to Food*, Penguin Books, 1999.

Dorenburg, Andrew and Page, Karen, *Culinary Artistry*, John Wiley & Sons Inc., 1996.

Helou, Anissa, *Mediterranean Street Food*, HarperCollins, 2002.

Henry, Diana, *Crazy Water, Pickled Lemons*, Mitchell Beazley, 2002.

Selby, Anna, *The Juice and Zest Book*, Collins and Brown, 2000.

Wheater, Caroline, *Juicing for Health*, HarperCollins, 2001.

Index